BARRON'S

WILLIAM SHAKESPEARE'S

Julius Caesar

BY
Michael Spring

SERIES EDITOR
Michael Spring
Editor, *Literary Cavalcade*
Scholastic Inc.

BARRON'S

BARRON'S EDUCATIONAL SERIES, INC.

For Betsy

ACKNOWLEDGMENTS

We would like to thank Loreto Todd, Senior Lecturer in English, University of Leeds, England, for preparing the chapter on Elizabethan English in this book.

We would like to acknowledge the many painstaking hours of work Holly Hughes and Thomas F. Hirsch have devoted to making the *Book Notes* series a success.

All inquiries should be addressed to:
Barron's Educational Series, Inc.
250 Wireless Boulevard
Hauppauge, New York 11788

Library of Congress Catalog Card No. 84-18473

International Standard Book No. 0-8120-3423-6

Library of Congress Cataloging in Publication Data
Spring, Michael.
  William Shakespeare's Julius Caesar.

  (Barron's book notes)
  Bibliography: p. 112
  Summary: A guide to reading "Julius Caesar" with a
critical and appreciative mind. Includes background on
the author's life and times, sample tests, term paper
suggestions, and a reading list.
  1. Shakespeare, William, 1564–1616. Julius Caesar.
2. Caesar, Julius, in fiction, drama, poetry, etc.
[1. Shakespeare, William, 1564–1616. Julius Caesar.
2. English literature—History and criticism] I. Title.
PR2808.S68   1984   822.3'3   84-18473
ISBN 0-8120-3423-6 (pbk.)

PRINTED IN THE UNITED STATES OF AMERICA

3   550   9876

CONTENTS

ADVISORY BOARD

HOW TO USE THIS BOOK

You have to know how to approach literature in order to get the most out of it. This *Barron's Book Notes* volume follows a plan based on methods used by some of the best students to read a work of literature.

Begin with the guide's section on the author's life and times. As you read, try to form a clear picture of the author's personality, circumstances, and motives for writing the work. This background usually will make it easier for you to hear the author's tone of voice, and follow where the author is heading.

Then go over the rest of the introductory material—such sections as those on the plot, characters, setting, themes, and style of the work. Underline, or write down in your notebook, particular things to watch for, such as contrasts between characters and repeated literary devices. At this point, you may want to develop a system of symbols to use in marking your text as you read. (Of course, you should only mark up a book you own, not one that belongs to another person or a school.) Perhaps you will want to use a different letter for each character's name, a different number for each major theme of the book, a different color for each important symbol or literary device. Be prepared to mark up the pages of your book as you read. Put your marks in the margins so you can find them again easily.

Now comes the moment you've been waiting for—the time to start reading the work of literature. You may want to put aside your *Barron's Book Notes* volume until you've read the work all the way through. Or you may want to alternate, reading the *Book Notes* analysis of each section as soon as you have finished reading the corresponding part of the original. Before you move on, reread crucial passages you don't fully understand. (Don't take this guide's analysis for granted—make up your own mind as to what the work means.)

Once you've finished the whole work of literature, you may want to review it right away, so you can firm up your ideas about what it means. You may want to leaf through the book concentrating on passages you marked in reference to one character or one theme. This is also a good time to reread the *Book Notes* introductory material, which pulls together insights on specific topics.

When it comes time to prepare for a test or to write a paper, you'll already have formed ideas about the work. You'll be able to go back through it, refreshing your memory as to the author's exact words and perspective, so that you can support your opinions with evidence drawn straight from the work. Patterns will emerge, and ideas will fall into place; your essay question or term paper will almost write itself. Give yourself a dry run with one of the sample tests in the guide. These tests present both multiple-choice and essay questions. An accompanying section gives answers to the multiple-choice questions as well as suggestions for writing the essays. If you have to select a term paper topic, you may choose one from the list of suggestions in this book. This guide also provides you with a reading list, to help you when you start research for a term paper, and a selection of provocative comments by critics, to spark your thinking before you write.

THE AUTHOR AND HIS TIMES

Julius Caesar is a play about a political assassination. The question it asks is: is it ever right to use force to remove a ruler from power? You, as readers, can answer that question in terms of your own experience in the last quarter of the 20th century. But if you're going to figure out what Shakespeare thought, you'll have to know something about the values and concerns of the Elizabethan world in which he lived.

History plays were popular during Shakespeare's lifetime (1564–1616) because this was the Age of Discovery, and English men and women were hungry to learn about worlds other than their own. But the Elizabethans also saw history as a mirror in which to discover themselves and find answers to the problems of their lives. A play like *Julius Caesar* taught the Elizabethans about Roman politics; it also offered an object lesson in how to live. What was Shakespeare trying to teach his contemporaries?

To answer that question, let's take a look at Elizabethan attitudes toward (a) monarchy and (b) order.

(A) MONARCHY

Today we believe in democracy and are suspicious of anyone who seeks unlimited power. We know what can happen when a Hitler or a Stalin takes control of a government, and we know just how corrupting power can be. But Shakespeare and his contemporaries had no such prejudice against strong rulers.

Their queen, Elizabeth I, ruled with an iron hand for forty-five years (from 1558 to 1603), yet her subjects had great affection for her. Under her rule the arts flourished and the economy prospered. While the rest of Europe was embroiled in war, mostly between Catholics and Protestants, England enjoyed a period relatively free from civil strife. Elizabeth's reign—and the reign of other Tudor monarchs, beginning with Henry VII in 1485—brought an end to the anarchy that had been England's fate during the Wars of the Roses (1455–84). To Shakespeare and his contemporaries the message was clear: only a strong, benevolent ruler could protect the peace and save the country from plunging into chaos again. Shakespeare would probably not have approved of the murder of Caesar.

(B) ORDER

In 1599, when *Julius Caesar* was first performed, Elizabeth was old and failing. She had never married and had no children to succeed her. Shakespeare and his contemporaries must have worried greatly that someone (like Brutus? like Cassius?) would try to grab power and plunge the country into civil war.

When the Elizabethans spoke of order, they didn't just mean political or social order. Though they lived during what we call today the English Renaissance, they still held many medieval views about man and his relation to the universe. They knew the world was round, and that the earth was one of many planets spinning in space. And they knew from explorers that there were continents besides their own. But most believed, as people in the Middle Ages believed, that the universe was ruled by a benevolent God, and that everything, from the lowest flower to the angels on high, had a divine purpose to fulfill. The king's right to rule came from God himself, and opposition to the king earned the wrath of God and threw the whole system into disorder. Rulers had responsibilities, too, of course: if they didn't work for the good of the people, God would hold them to account. No one in this essentially medieval world lived or functioned in isolation. Everyone was linked together by a chain of rights and obligations, and when someone broke that chain, the whole system broke down and plunged the world into chaos. What destroys the divine harmony in *Julius Caesar*—Cassius' jealousy, Caesar's ambition, or the fickleness of the mob—is something you'll have to decide for yourself. But whatever the cause, the results offend the heavens and throw the entire country into disarray.

Today a sense of hopelessness and despair hangs over us: a mistake, a simple misunderstanding, and the bomb may drop and destroy life on earth. Our fate, we feel, is out of our control. But the Elizabethans were much more optimistic. Forget chance: if something went wrong, then someone had broken God's laws, the laws of the universe. Many would suffer, but in the end the guilty would be punished and order restored.

Julius Caesar begins with a human act that, like a virus, infects the body of the Roman state. No one is untouched; some grow sick, some die. But in time the poison works its way out of the system and the state grows healthy again. In Shakespeare's world, health, not sickness, is the natural condition of man in God's divine plan.

THE PLAY

The Plot

The working people of Rome are overjoyed: Julius Caesar has beaten Pompey's sons in battle, and everyone's getting a day off from work to celebrate Caesar's triumphant return. But two Roman officers, Flavius and Marullus, chase the crowds away: how dare the citizens support a tyrant who threatens to undermine hundreds of years of Republican (representative) rule! Don't they know that Caesar wants to be king?

Caesar parades by in full glory, just in time to help celebrate the races on the Feast of Lupercal. A soothsayer bids him "Beware the ides of March" (March 15), but Caesar—anxious not to show fear in public—dismisses the man as a dreamer. The procession passes by, leaving behind two Roman Senators: Cassius, a long-time political enemy of Caesar, and Brutus, Caesar's friend. Like other members of the Senate, Brutus and Cassius are aristocrats who fear that Caesar will take away their ancient privileges.

Cassius now goes to work on Brutus, flattering him, reminding him of his noble ancestry, trying all the while to determine just how unhappy Brutus is with Caesar and just how willing Brutus is to join the conspiracy. Does Brutus know where Cassius is leading him? It's hard to tell. Brutus admits only that he's dissatisfied, and agrees to discuss the matter further.

Caesar, now back from the races, tells his friend Antony that he doesn't trust a man like Cassius, with his "lean and hungry look." He has good reason to be suspicious!

Casca tells Brutus and Cassius how the Roman people three times offered Caesar the crown, and how three times he refused it. Perhaps Caesar doesn't want to be king—that's what his friends would argue; but to his enemies, Caesar was merely playing on the gullibility of the people, pretending to be humble in order to win their support.

On a stormy night full of mysterious omens, Cassius converts Casca to his cause and arranges for Cinna, a fellow-conspirator, to throw a message through Brutus' window. The note will, he hopes, win the noble Senator to their side.

Alone in his garden, Brutus tries to justify the part he is about to play in the murder of his friend, Caesar. He decides finally that Caesar's ambition poses a grave danger to the future of the Republic and that Caesar should be destroyed, not for what he is, but for what he's likely to become. The conspirators arrive at Brutus' house and agree to murder Caesar the next day at the Capitol. They would like to murder Antony, too, but Brutus, anxious to keep his hands clean and to preserve his precious honor, insists that Antony be spared.

After the conspirators leave, Brutus' wife Portia enters. She wants to know what's happening. Brutus worries that the news may be too frightening for her to bear, but nevertheless confides in her.

Caesar has had a restless night, too. His wife Calpurnia tries to keep him home—she senses evil in the air—and at first he relents. But the conspirators arrive and pursuade him to go to the Senate as planned. What would happen to his reputation if his public thought the mighty Caesar was swayed by a superstitious wife!

Calpurnia's fears turn out to be more than superstitions, for the day is March 15, the ides of March. Caesar ignores two more warnings and, after delivering a speech full of extravagant self-praise, he is stabbed by the conspirators and dies.

Antony, learning of the murder of his dearest friend, begs the conspirators to let him speak at the funeral. Believing that right is on his side, Brutus agrees, over the objections of his more realistic friends. Left alone, Antony vows to revenge the death of Caesar, even if it means plunging his country into civil war. In the meantime, Caesar's adopted son and heir, Octavius, has arrived on the outskirts of Rome, and Antony advises him to wait there till he can gauge the mood of the country.

Brutus' funeral oration ia a measured, well-reasoned speech, appealing to the better instincts of the people and to their abstract sense of duty to the state. For a moment he wins them over. But then Antony inflames the crowds with an appeal to their emotions. Showing them Caesar's bloody clothes turns them into an angry mob, hungry for revenge. Blind with hate, they roam the streets and tear apart the innocent poet Cinna.

Antony and Octavius now join forces with Lepidus to pursue and destroy the conspirators, who have fled from Rome. Anyone who might endanger their cause is coldly put to death. Brutus and Cassius await this new triumverate at their camp near Sardis in Asia Minor. Should Cassius let an officer take bribes? Brutus, standing on his principles, says no, and vents his anger on his friend. At the root of his anger, however, is his unspoken sorrow at the death of his beloved wife Portia. Apparently unable to deal with such an unsettling situation, she went mad and took her life by swallowing hot coals. Sadness over her death brings Brutus and Cassius back together again, closer perhaps than before.

At night Brutus is visited by the ghost of Caesar, who vows to meet him again on the battlefield at Philippi in Greece. The next day the two armies—the army of Brutus and Cassius, and the army of Antony and Octavius—stand in readiness at Phillipi while the four generals battle each other with words. In the first encounter, Brutus' troops defeat Octavius', and Antony's troops overcome Cassius'. Cassius, retreating to a nearby hill, sends his trusted friend Titinius to find out whether approaching troops are friends or foes. Is Titinius captured? It appears so; and Cassius, believing he has sent his good friend to his death and that the battle is lost, takes his life.

If only Cassius hadn't acted so rashly he might have saved his life, for the reports turn out to be false and Titinius still lives. Brutus, not the enemy, arrives, and mourns the death of his friend.

The tide now turns against Brutus. Sensing defeat, and unwilling to endure the dishonor of capture, he runs on his sword and dies. Like Caesar and Cassius, he thinks in his final moments not of power or personal glory, but of friendship.

Antony delivers a eulogy over Brutus' body, calling him "the noblest Roman of them all." Octavius agrees to take all of Brutus' men into his service, a gesture of reconciliation that bodes well for the future.

The Characters

JULIUS CAESAR

In order to discuss Shakespeare's play intelligently you have to make up your mind about (1) Caesar's character, and (2) Caesar's threat to the Roman Republic. Either Caesar deserves to be assassinated, or he doesn't. On your answer hangs the meaning of the play.

On one hand, Caesar is a tyrant whose ambition poses a real danger to the Republic. In that case, the hero of the play is Brutus. On the other hand, Caesar may be vain and arrogant, but he is the only ruler strong enough to hold the Roman Republic together, and a flawed ruler is better than none at all. In that case, Brutus becomes an impractical idealist who is manipulated by a group of scheming politicians.

Whatever your position, there's no doubt that Shakespeare wants to show us the private side of a public man, and to remind us that our heroes are, like the rest of us, only human. In public, Caesar is worshipped like a god; in private, he is superstitious, deaf, and subject to fits of epilepsy (falling sickness). Caesar's public image is like a mask he wears to hide his weaknesses from others and from himself. Yet at the moment of death his mask slips, and we see another Caesar who values friendship above all.

Let's look at Caesar in three different ways.

1. Caesar's personal shortcomings are one reason to remove him from power. Another is his ambition, which threatens to undermine the power of the people and their elected representatives.

It's true that Antony calls Caesar "the noblest man/ That ever lived in the tide of times" (*Act III, Scene i, lines 256-257*), but why believe Antony—a man blindly devoted to his master, who is so bad a judge of character that he says of Cassius:

> Fear him not, Caesar, he's not dangerous;
> *Act I, Scene ii, line 196*

Caesar's refusal to accept the crown is no more than a cynical political gesture to impress the masses. His speech comparing himself to the North Star is the height of arrogance and blasphemy. His refusal to pardon Publius Cimber is the mark of a man incapable of justice or pity. Such a man is a tyrant who knows no limits and deserves to be destroyed.

2. Caesar may be ambitious, but what of it? Ambition in itself is neither good nor bad. Today, in our democratic age, we are suspicious of politicians who seek unlimited power, but the Elizabethans in Shakespeare's time lived under a strong monarchy and would have had no such prejudice against strong rulers. If Shakespeare had wanted to show that Caesar was unfit to rule, he could have found evidence to support that point of view in Elizabethan history books; but nowhere in the play does he show Caesar suppressing civil liberties. Brutus himself is forced to admit:

> and, to speak truth of Caesar,
> I have not known when his affections swayed
> More than his reason.
> *Act II, Scene i, lines 19-21*

A politician should be judged for his accomplishments, not for his private life. Even if Caesar is inflexible, the times demand such behavior.

In his personal life, Caesar is considerate to his wife, courteous to the conspirators, and generous to the Roman people. He may be vain, but he has something to be vain about. Friends and enemies alike praise his courage and his accomplishments on the battlefield—can they all be wrong?

3.   Caesar may be neither a hero nor a villain, but, like people in real life, a mixture of both. Educated theater-goers in Shakespeare's time had this double image of Caesar, and Shakespeare may have enjoyed reinforcing and undercutting their preconceptions without ever resolving them.

Shakespeare had one other reason to make Caesar a mixture of good and evil: if Caesar were too noble, Brutus would become a simple villain; if Caesar were too evil, Brutus would become a simple hero. In either case the moral dilemma raised by the assassination would no longer exist.

How you yourself react to Caesar will perhaps say as much about you as it says about him. People with a strong need for political order in their lives may want to defend him. Those of you with a more democratic faith in the individual may prefer to see him as a threat to the people, and sympathize with Brutus.

BRUTUS

Scholars, actors, students—all have disagreed about Brutus and will continue to disagree as long as *Julius Caesar* is being read and performed.

You can view Brutus as a man of high principles and integrity—a man who is defeated, not by any personal shortcomings, but by the underhandedness of Cassius, the fickleness of the mob, and the inevita-

ble march of Roman history from a republic to a monarchy.

You can also see Brutus as a windbag—an unfeeling, self-righteous bore who cloaks his evil deeds in
high principles and plunges his country into civil
war.

Which is the "real" Brutus? It depends in part on
whether you think the assassination was necessary. It
also depends on whether you think Brutus uses language to convey the truth, or to hide from it. Take
these lines of his:

> For let the gods so speed me, as I love
> The name of honor more than I fear death.
> *Act I, Scene ii, lines 88-89*

Brutus thinks he is telling the truth—but is he?
Would a truly honorable man need to call attention to
his honor?

One point is indisputable: Brutus believes in his
principles, and his principles do, to some extent, control his behavior. He stands apart from all the other
characters in the way he is influenced by ideas, rather
than by feelings or the wish for personal gain. Cassius
assassinates Caesar because he is jealous of him; Brutus acts only for what he considers the best interests of
the state. Antony is a man of action who pauses only
to consider the best way of getting from A to B; Brutus
is a man of ideas who weighs his behavior in terms of
Right and Wrong. Antony believes that brute strength
and passion rule the world, and manipulates people
accordingly; Brutus believes that reason rules the
world, and that people can be swayed by the power of
truth and logic. Cassius and Antony see life as a game
or competition in which rewards go to the strongest or

swiftest; Brutus sees life as a confrontation of ideas in which rewards go to the just. He is such a private and self-contained man that he won't even share the news of his wife's death with his good friend Cassius.

Brutus is high-minded, but his principles do not seem to prepare him very well for dealing with a corrupt world. He cannot recognize motives that are less noble than his own, and is therefore preyed upon by unscrupulous politicians. As Cassius himself says behind Brutus' back:

> Well, Brutus, thou art noble; yet I see
> Thy honorable mettle may be wrought
> From that it is disposed; therefore it is meet
> That noble minds keep ever with their likes;
> For who so firm that cannot be seduced?
>   *Act I, Scene ii, lines 308-312*

Brutus' principles force him to spare Antony's life and to let Antony speak at Caesar's funeral. His own speech lacks power (compared to Antony's) because he assumes that people can be led by reason. An honorable man, he uses language to communicate the truth rather than to stir up the emotions of the people; he doesn't understand that people *want* to be led—if not by Caesar, then by someone else.

Some readers see Brutus as a bookish man who can function only in a world of ideas. True, he is not much of a politician; but is it fair to describe him as a man whose head is in the clouds? Cassius, after all, is constantly asking and taking his advice. It is Brutus who calls for action and who takes the offensive at Philippi; and it is Brutus, not Antony, who wins the battle. Brutus does make some unwise decisions, but does that mean he is incapable of functioning in the world?

Almost all the characters in *Julius Caesar* struggle to be better than they are, and Brutus is no exception. He, too, falls short of his ideals. Although he insists on living by the loftiest principles, Cassius gets him to join the conspiracy by flattering him and appealing to his sense of family pride.

Brutus tries to live by reason alone, yet he cannot sleep at night, and is so plagued by a guilty conscience that Caesar's ghost appears to him in a dream. In his argument with Cassius, Brutus is reduced to a squabbling child—perhaps because he is mad with grief (though he tries not to show it) over the death of his wife. In the end Brutus takes his own life, in violation of his Stoic philosophy, which demands that he accept whatever fate holds in store for him. Is Brutus a hero, then—or is he a villain? Let's look at him in both lights.

1.   Brutus is a man who cares more about principles than people—who uses principles to justify the murder of a friend. He is so blinded by ideals that he cannot see into his own heart, or recognize the needs of the world. He is a moral snob who dislikes debate or compromise and always insists on getting his own way.

This Brutus knows exactly what Cassius is up to, but lets himself be led in order to keep his own hands clean. He is a hypocrite who hides behind lofty principles and pretty phrases. Despite his reputation for honor, he is easily flattered and concerned about his reputation. His pride causes him to dismiss Cicero—a potential rival—even though Cicero is the greatest orator of the times.

In his refusal to accept his human limitations, Brutus is as vain and dangerous as Caesar.

2.   Brutus is simply too noble for the world he lives in. He sacrifices his friend Caesar to do what is best for his country. He remains faithful to his principles to the end. Everyone, even Caesar, admires him and seeks his friendship. He is a tragic figure only because he tries to be better than he can, and fails.

Hero or villain—could Brutus possibly be both? Does the world need more men of principle, or less? Shakespeare forces us to ask these questions, but lets us find answers for ourselves.

CASSIUS

There are many sides to Cassius. This makes him difficult to pin down or sum up in a phrase—but it also makes him true to life.

Here are two opinions of Cassius. From Caesar:

> Yond Cassius has a lean and hungry look;
> He thinks too much: such men are dangerous.
> *Act I, Scene ii, lines 194–195*

From Brutus:

> The last of all the Romans, fare thee well!
> It is impossible that ever Rome
> Should breed thy fellow [equal].
> *Act V, Scene iii, lines 99–101*

Both judgments are true—and false, for Cassius is different men to different people. Depending on how a person treats him, he can be loving or ruthless, gentle or hard, passionate or aloof. One moment he is deceiving his dear friend Brutus; the next, he is craving affection from him.

When we first meet Cassius, he is busy lying, flattering, forging letters, subverting the principles of his good friend Brutus. Caesar's opinion of him seems right on target. He's not motivated by the best interests of Rome, but by the desire for revenge on a man who doesn't like him. Jealousy moves him—jealousy of the fame and power of a man he considers no more worthy than himself.

Caesar calls Cassius a "lean and hungry" man, and you may want to take this as the final word on Cassius and interpret all his actions in this light. But Caesar's verdict is not the only one. Cassius' love for Brutus, for instance, seems quite genuine—particularly after the assassination. Cassius has many admirers and friends who are willing to fight and die for him. After the argument with Brutus, Cassius shows good-natured tolerance for the Poet. As death approaches, Cassius realizes that he is not the measure of all things, and that there are forces at work in the universe beyond his understanding and control. He takes his life , not because he has lost the battle, but because he believes (mistakenly) that he has caused the death of a friend.

Almost everything Cassius says and does, both before and after the assassination, can be interpreted as a direct, emotional reaction to people. He responds to people as Brutus responds to ideas. Whether he is conspiring to kill Caesar or asking for Brutus' love, Cassius is motivated by a boyish need for affection, and by a boyish hatred of those who refuse it. His reasons for killing Caesar seem to be strictly personal. Caesar, his close boyhood friend, has rejected him. "Caesar doth bear me hard," he says—Caesar bears a grudge against me and therefore must be destroyed.

When Cassius meets Brutus, he is disturbed by the absence of "that gentleness/And show of love as I was wont [accustomed] to have" *(Act I, Scene ii, lines 33–34)*. In the quarrel scene, Cassius tells Brutus, like a pouting child, "You love me not" *(Act IV, Scene iii, line 88)*. What upsets Cassius most are not Brutus' accusations but the fact that Brutus does not have "love enough" to bear with him.

Cassius' spitefulness and his craving for affection are childlike. He seems genuinely perplexed that Caesar, a man no stronger than himself, could become so powerful. He behaves like a boy who discovers that his idol has clay feet, and destroys it rather than live with its imperfections. "Such men as he be never at heart's ease" *(Act I, Scene ii, line 208)*, says Caesar.

If you reread Cassius' speech against Caesar *(Act I, Scene ii, lines 90–161)*, you'll see how Cassius equates worthiness with such traditionally masculine traits as physical strength and endurance. Perhaps because he has so little sense of himself, and of his own worth, he suffers from a sensitive ego, and measures himself not against some abstract standards of right and wrong (as Brutus does), but against others.

Cassius blames himself for giving Caesar so much power:

> The fault, dear Brutus, is not in our stars,
> But in ourselves, that we are underlings.
> *Act I, Scene ii, lines 140–141*

These are the words of a spiritual outcast, who sees himself alone in the universe. Only as death nears does Cassius recognize himself as part of a divine plan, and achieve some measure of peace.

Cassius, we learn from Caesar, "hears no music."

Here's what Lorenzo in Shakespeare's play *The Merchant of Venice* says about his type:

> The man that hath no music in himself,
> Nor is not mov'd with concord of sweet sounds,
> Is fit for treasons, stratagems, and spoils;
> The motions of his spirit are dull as night,
> And his affections dark as Erebus.
> Let no such man be trusted
>   *Act V, Scene i, Lines 83–88*

To Shakespeare, an inability to hear music was, quite literally, an inability to hear the harmonies of the universe. The fact that Cassius hears no music does not in itself make him evil, but it does reveal a lack of inner harmony, and a restlessness that can never be satisfied.

Cassius and Caesar are enemies in life, but the two are almost indistinguishable at the moment of death. Both let their masks slip, and reveal the gentleness that lies beneath. At this moment of truth, there is no masculine talk of revenge—no war cries or curses—but a simple lament for the betrayal of friends.

ANTONY

There are many "Antonys." One of them is passionate and impulsive; the other is in complete control of his emotions. One can cry over the death of his dear friend Caesar; the other condemns his associates to death without batting an eyelash. One makes a powerful political speech with perfect understanding of human nature; the other can be so mistaken about human nature that he calls Cassius "not dangerous."

Can such opposites exist within the same man? It's possible that Shakespeare couldn't make up his mind about Antony, and painted an unfinished portrait of him. It's also possible that Shakespeare was trying to portray the many sides of an opportunist. An opportunist is a person who adjusts his values to suit his purposes; who uses people and events to get what he wants, regardless of principles or consequences. If Antony is such a man, it is understandable that, like a chameleon, he would change colors from one moment to the next.

How different Antony is from Brutus! Brutus stands behind his principles, refusing to be swayed by circumstance; Antony never lets principles stand in the way of success. Brutus' conscience keeps him up at night; tactics, manoeuvres, schemes—these are what concern Antony.

A modern man, Antony takes the world as he finds it and uses whatever means are necessary to get what he wants. Life for him is a game—serious, but a game nonetheless—and he is a skillful player who knows how to win.

Antony is an opportunist, yes, but is he evil? Look closely at his words and actions, and you can find evidence to support that point of view. In his famous funeral oration, for instance, nothing could be more offensive than the way he fires up the masses by appealing to their basest emotions. And nothing could be more irresponsible than the way he unleases the "dogs of war"—bringing death and destruction to innocent and guilty alike.

Antony is cynical, callous and unprincipled, yet he is motivated not by personal ambition but by the desire to revenge the death of a friend. His almost dog-like devotion to Caesar reveals a deep capacity for loyalty and affection. He is cunning, but, unlike Brutus, completely honest with himself. He may manipulate people, but he speaks with conviction, and what he says is deeply felt. His funeral oration is more effective than Brutus' because he speaks from the heart.

In the end, Antony (with Octavius' help), triumphs. Is Shakespeare suggesting that realists like Antony are the hope of the future? Perhaps Shakespeare is merely pointing out that Antony and his kind are more likely to succeed in a world as imperfect as the one we live in.

OCTAVIUS

Octavius—Caesar's adopted son—is more important a character than his appearances (only four) and his lines (only 30) would indicate, since the fate of Rome rests in his hands after the death of the conspirators. From such limited information, we have to decide whether Rome has been left in good hands.

What we should be able to agree on is this: Octavius is a capable soldier who accomplishes the work at hand by whatever means are needed to achieve it. Honorable men like Brutus can be dangerous; perhaps Rome needs pragmatists like Octavius to reestablish order.

The first time Octavius appears *(Act IV, Scene i, line 2)* he is busy checking off names of people who must die—including the brother of his friend Lepidus. Is he a coldblooded murderer, then? Perhaps. But he is also a hardened soldier, who knows that it is sometimes necessary to sacrifice individuals for the sake of victory. Like Brutus, he kills for what he considers the greater good; but, unlike Brutus, he has no qualms about it.

Moments later *(Act IV, Scene i, lines 27–28)*, Octavius tries to save Lepidus' life. Since he showed no mercy to Lepidus' brother, we can assume he is not just being a good guy, but that he recognizes the practical value of having a "tried and valiant soldier" in his ranks.

Yet Octavius lets Antony decide Lepidus' fate. Is this a sign of weakness? Or is it the wise decision of a practical man, who knows the issue isn't worth fighting over?

The second time Octavius appears *(Act V, Scene i, lines 1–20)*, he ignores Antony's wishes and insists on keeping his forces to the right side of the battlefield. "I do not cross you," he tells Antony, "but I will do so." Octavius seems to be behaving like a willful young Caesar, insisting on his natural right to rule. Whether his tone is spiteful, or firm but polite, you'll have to decide for yourself.

Only moments later *(line 24)*, Octavius asks Antony if they should attack, and this time he gives in to Antony's wishes. Once again you'll have to decide: is Octavius incapable of important decisions—or is he simply smart enough to listen to someone with more experience?

The four generals now confront each other before the battle *(lines 27–66)*—Octavius and Antony on one side, Brutus and Cassius on the other. Antony, Brutus and Cassius squabble like children—only Octavius keeps his perspective. "Come, come, the cause," he says—let's keep our sights on what's important and get to the matter at hand.

The third time we see Octavius *(Act V, Scene v, line 60)*, he offers to take all of Brutus' men into his service. This may be an act of charity, but from what we know of Octavius, he is probably motivated by the practical need to end the war and bring both sides together under his single rule. His intentions may not matter so much as the fact that he is trying to end the bloodshed and reestablish order.

As the successor to Caesar, Octavius is given the final words of the play. It is as a soldier, not as a noble man, that Octavius praises Brutus, for nobility is a quality Octavius seems indifferent to. His tribute to Brutus may not be genuine—he is probably only doing what is expected of him—but whatever his motives, he seems to have no interest in revenge. His desire to reunite the country bodes well for the future of Rome.

(The historic Octavius did restore order. He also restored the Republic—but more in name than in fact. The Senate retained its forms and privileges, but the power resided in Octavius, who controlled the army. In 27 B.C. Antony took the name of Augustus and became the first Roman Emperor. Shakespeare portrays him principally as a soldier, yet during his reign he became more interested in peace than in war, and his rule became known as the golden age of Roman literature and architecture.)

PORTIA

There are two ways to view Portia. Let's look at them.

1. Portia is often seen today as a champion of women's rights—a feminist living nearly four centuries ahead of her time.

According to this view, Portia is a woman who demands equality with her husband. She insists on being treated as an individual, not as an object or an idea. She speaks of herself and Brutus as "one" (*Act II, Scene i, lines 261–278*), and of Brutus himself as "your self, your half." She demands to know his secret, however painful it may be. She will not be condescended to; she will not be treated as a child.

This Portia is strong-willed but modest, dignified but tender. She is one of the few characters in the play who uses language to communicate the truth rather than to hide from it. She has an innate sense of wisdom that lets her see through words to the very heart of things. (When Brutus attributes his moodiness to bad health, for instance, Portia immediately knows he is lying to protect her.) Though Portia is high-minded and independent, she is also a loving and devoted wife, who kills herself rather than live alone.

2. That is one view of Portia—there is another.

According to this less flattering view, Portia makes the mistake of trying to be more than a woman, fails miserably, and brings about her own destruction.

Portia points proudly to her self-inflicted wound (*Act II, Scene i, lines 299–302*) to prove to Brutus just how capable she is of functioning in a world of men. She also prides herself on being the daughter of Cato, a man famous for his integrity, who took his own life rather than be taken prisoner (in the civil war between Caesar and Pompey). Says Portia:

> Think you I am no stronger than my sex,
> Being so fathered and so husbanded?
> > *Act II, Scene i, lines 296–297*

Brutus takes her at her word, confides his secret to

her, and what happens? Portia goes mad with grief, and eventually takes her own life.

Portia's mistake is to confuse her private self with her public image as Cato's daughter. Like Brutus and Caesar, she tries to live up to her name and be someone she is not—with disastrous results. In her death—as in Brutus' and Caesar's—we see the danger of wearing a public mask, and forgetting whom we are underneath.

Note that Portia wants to be Brutus' equal only so that she can be more a part of *his* life; nowhere does she suggest that she expects him to be part of hers. The very fact of losing him drives her mad. Portia thus sums herself up best:

> Ay me, how weak a thing
> The heart of woman is!
> *Act II, Scene iv, lines 39–40*

Is this Shakespeare's unhappy view of women, and the final word on Portia? Or are the other critics right—the ones who see her as the ideal, modern woman, who dies for love?

Either interpretation can be correct—depending on how you choose to view her.

CALPURNIA

Caesar's wife speaks only 26 lines, so we never get to know her very well.

There are at least two ways to view her—one of them more flattering than the other.

On one hand, she is undignified, nervous, and weak. She is also superstitious and haunted by unreasonable fears, and Caesar cannot be blamed for treating her like a child.

On the other hand, Calpurnia is a devoted wife—as concerned about Caesar's well-being as Portia is about Brutus'. True, she has strange dreams, but all of them come true. Perhaps in her intuitive, female way she is closer to the truth than Caesar.

Whichever way you view Calpurnia, you will have to admit that her relationship with Caesar is less than ideal.

Calpurnia's talk with Caesar follows closely on Portia's meeting with Brutus, as if Shakespeare were drawing attention to the differences between the two relationships.

Portia greets her husband with respect as "my lord" (*Act II, Scene i, line 234*). She may be flattering him to get what she wants, but she at least follows the forms of courtesy. Brutus is as concerned about her health as she is about his.

How does Calpurnia greet Caesar? With an order:

> Think you to walk forth?
> You shall not stir out of your house today.
> *Act II, Scene ii, lines 8–9*

And Caesar replies:

> Caesar shall forth.

Calpurnia is foolish enough to turn her request into a battle of wills. She makes the mistake of treating her husband in public as the mortal he is; and Caesar, to preserve his public image, has to take a stand against her.

Caesar, of course, has been equally tactless or unfeeling—announcing to all the world (*Act I, Scene ii, lines 6–9*) that his wife is sterile.

Can you blame a wife for treating her husband as a mortal and not as a god? The fact that she can see the man behind the mask points up her strength—or her weakness.

Other Elements
SETTING

All scenes through Act IV, Scene i are set in Rome. Act IV, Scenes ii and iii, take place near Sardis in Asia Minor. All of Act V is set near the plains of Philippi in Greece. The play begins on February 15, 44 B.C., on the Feast of Lupercal; continues through the assassination of Caesar a month later; and concludes with the Battle of Philippi in 42 B.C., when Brutus and Cassius commit suicide and Caesar's heir, Octavius, assumes power. Shakespeare, of course, was a dramatist, not a playwright, and in order to preserve the dramatic unity of the action he telescoped a period of three years into six days.

THEMES

Here is a list of the major themes of *Julius Caesar*. They will be studied in depth in the scene-by-scene discussion of the play. Notice that some themes contradict each other—since critics disagree, it's up to you to decide which ones are true. This book will help you find evidence to support your position.

1. A PORTRAIT OF CAESAR OR OF BRUTUS

Caesar

The play is a portrait of Caesar—why else would Shakespeare name the play after him? Though Caesar is killed in the third act, his spirit—what he stands for—dominates the action of the play until Brutus' death, and then is reborn in the person of Octavius.

Brutus

The play is a portrait of Brutus—why else would Shakespeare end the play with Brutus' death, and with the opposition's tributes to him? Brutus is studied in greater depth than any other character, and the action of the play revolves around his role in the assassination. Shakespeare called his play *Julius Caesar* only because he was writing about the period in Roman history when Caesar reigned.

2.   FRIENDSHIP

Friendship is at the center of Shakespeare's vision of an ordered, harmonious world. Disloyalty and distrust cause this world to crumble. Relationships suffer when people put their principles ahead of their affections, and when they let their roles as public officials interfere with their private lives. As death approaches, characters forget their worldly ambitions, and speak about the loyalty of friends.

3.   LANGUAGE

We think of language as a way of sharing our thoughts and feelings, and of communicating the truth; but in *Julius Caesar* people use language to disguise their thoughts and feelings, and to distort the truth. Language is used to humiliate and flatter. Words are powerful weapons that turn evil into good and throw an entire country into civil war.

4.   A STUDY OF HISTORY

Shakespeare is dramatizing an important period in Roman history, when Rome developed from a republic (with a representative form of government) to a monarchy (with a single ruler). He is not blaming or praising anyone, but objectively portraying the major factors that contributed to this development: Caesar's ambition; the frustrations of a weakened and divided Senate; and the needs and wishes of the Roman people.

5. THE PRIVATE LIVES OF PUBLIC FIGURES

We like to think that our political heroes are free from ordinary human weaknesses. Shakespeare reminds us that behind their masks of fame are mortals like the rest of us—with the same prejudices, physical handicaps, hopes, and fears. When these public figures try to live up to their own self-images, they bring destruction on themselves, and on the world.

6. FATE AND THE SUPERNATURAL

A sense of fate hangs over the events in *Julius Caesar*—a sense that the assassination is inevitable and that the fortunes of the characters have been determined in advance. The characters are foolish to ignore prophecies and omens, which invariably come true; yet they are free to act as though the future were unknown. They are the playthings of powers they can neither understand nor control, yet they are held accountable for everything they do.

7. PRAGMATISTS AND MEN OF PRINCIPLE

Shakespeare is comparing two types of people: the man of fixed moral standards, who expects others to be as honorable as himself; and the pragmatist, who accepts the world for what it is and does everything necessary to achieve his goals. The pragmatist is less admirable, but more effective. Shakespeare is either *(a)* pointing out the uselessness of morals and principles in a corrupt world, or *(b)* dramatizing the tragedy of a noble man destroyed by a world less perfect than he is.

8. THE ASSASSINATION
The Murder Is Just
A ruler forfeits his right to rule when he oversteps the heaven-appointed limits to his power. Caesar deserves to die on two counts: first, he considers himself an equal to the gods; and second, he threatens to undermine hundreds of years of republican (representative) rule. Brutus sacrifices his life to preserve the freedom of the people, and to save his country from the clutches of a tyrant.
The Murder Is Unjust
Shakespeare's contemporaries respected strong rulers, who could check the dangerous impulses of the masses and protect their country from civil war. They believed that order and stability were worth preserving at any price. Shakespeare's play may therefore be a warning against the use of violence to overthrow authority. The assassination destroys nothing but the conspirators themselves, since Caesar's spirit lives on in the hearts of the people.

STYLE

There's not much poetry in Julius Caesar. Perhaps because the action takes place in Rome, the characters all seem to speak like orators. On the battlefield, or even with friends, they're always making speeches! Read some of the longer ones aloud; you'll see how alike everyone sounds, how everyone speaks clearly and simply and says exactly what he thinks. The men in Shakespeare's play are politicians who avoid flowery language and metaphor; they express themselves often in one-syllable words strung together in simple, declarative sentences. This is the language of people who are—or who try to be—in control of their emotions, and who use words not to create beauty, but to manipulate each other and to get things done. Shakespeare may be using language to mirror the restrained and formal mood of classical Rome. Perhaps, too, he wants to show how people use language to mask their feelings from themselves and from others. As readers, we have to look beneath these masks and ask ourselves: who are these people? what do they really think, and what are they really saying?

SOURCES

Shakespeare found his basic material for *Julius Caesar* in *The Lives of the Noble Grecians and Romans,* written by a Greek named Plutarch in the first century after Christ. Plutarch, like Shakespeare, wrote history as a guide for his contemporaries. It's not surprising that Shakespeare was attracted to Plutarch, for Plutarch was more a biographer than an historian, and his tales are full of wonderful dramatic touches.

Shakespeare did not read Plutarch in Greek. *The Lives* was translated into French by Jacques Amyet in 1559 and then from French into English by Sir Thomas North in 1579. That was 20 years before the first production of *Julius Caesar.*

Plutarch wrote separate biographies of Julius Cae-

sar, Brutus, and Antony, and often gives three different accounts of the same events. It's fun to read these
biographies today to see which accounts Shakspeare
followed, which he ignored, and which he transformed for his own dramatic purposes. At times
Shakespeare lifted material directly from Plutarch.
Shakespeare's Caesar, for example, says:

> Yond Cassius has a lean and hungry look;
> He thinks too much: such men are dangerous.
> *Act 1, Scene ii, lines 194–195*

Notice how close that is to Plutarch's version:

> Caesar also had Cassius in great jealousy and sus-
> pected him much, whereupon he said on a time to
> his friends: "What will Cassius do, think ye? I like
> not his pale looks."

Plutarch's Brutus can do nothing wrong. Some of
you will want to argue that Shakespeare thought less
of Brutus; others will want to quote Plutarch to prove
that Shakespeare's Brutus was indeed a noble man.

As for Caesar, Plutarch's portrait is close to Shakespeare's: a ruler guilty of great pride and ambition, but
also a benefactor of the people.

Shakespeare's portrait of Caesar may also have
been influenced by Elizabethan attitudes toward him.
Some saw Caesar as a hero; others, as a tyrant and a
traitor. Shakespeare may have enjoyed exploiting
these differences, playing them against each other
without ever resolving them. Shakespeare may also
have drawn Caesar's portrait from the vain and boast-
ful heroes (such as Tamburlaine) brought to life on
stage during his lifetime.

AN HISTORICAL NOTE

When you think of Senators, you naturally think of elected representatives of the people. But in ancient Rome the Senate was made up of wealthy aristocrats and conservatives who sought to defend their ancient privileges. Caesar was a reformer who wanted to reduce the power of the Senate, and to share their lands and privileges with the common people.

Both Senators and reformers looked to the generals for support. Pompey represented the interests of the Senators; Caesar defended the reformers. In 47 B.C. Caesar crossed the Rubican and defeated Pompey; two years later he defeated Pompey's sons in Egypt. No wonder the Roman officers Flavius and Marullus (Act I, Scene i) are upset by Caesar's triumphant return from battle! And no wonder the common people are overjoyed! Caesar may have wanted to be king or dictator, but it was he, not the Senators, who had the interests of the people at heart. Perhaps that's why in Shakespeare's play we never see Caesar depriving the Romans of their civil liberties, or the Senators discussing what they'll do for the people of Rome once Caesar is destroyed.

ELIZABETHAN ENGLISH

All languages change. Differences in pronunciation and word choice are apparent even between parents and their children. If language differences can appear in one generation, it is only to be expected that the English used by Shakespeare four hundred years ago will diverge markedly from the English used today. The following information on Shakespeare's language will help a modern reader to a fuller understanding of *Julius Caesar*.

Mobility of Word Classes

Adjectives, nouns and verbs were less rigidly con-
fined to particular classes in Shakespeare's day. Verbs
were often used as nouns. In Act II, Scene ii, line 16
'watch' is used to mean 'watchmen':

> There is one within . . .
> Recounts most horrid sights seen by the watch.

Nouns could be used as adjectives as when cross is
used to mean crossed or forked:

> And when the cross blue lightning seemed to
>   open
> The breast of heaven . . . *(I, iii, 50)*

and as verbs as when 'joy' is used to mean 'rejoice':

> My heart doth joy *(V, v, 34)*.

Adjectives could be used as adverbs:

> . . . thou couldst not die more honourable *(V, i,
>   60)*,

as nouns:

> I'll about,
> And drive away the vulgar from the streets *(I, i,
>   72)*

'Vulgar' is the equivalent of 'common people'.

Changes in Word Meaning

The meanings of words undergo changes, a process
that can be illustrated by the fact that 'chip' extended
its meaning from a small piece of wood to a small
piece of silicon. Many of the words in Shakespeare
still exist today but their meanings have changed. The
change may be small, as in the case of 'modestly'
meaning 'without exaggeration' in:

I your glass
Will modestly discover to yourself . . . *(I, ii, 68–*
69)

or more fundamental, so that 'naughty' meant
'worthless' *(I, i, 15)*, 'tributaries' meant 'conquered
rulers who paid tribute' *(I, i, 35)*, 'shadow' meant 're-
flection' *(I, ii, 58)*, 'speed' meant 'prosper' *(I, ii, 88)*,
'temper' meant 'constitution' *(I, ii, 129)* and 'sad'
meant 'serious':

. . . Casca, tell us what hath chanced today
That Caesar looks so sad. *(I, ii, 217)*

Vocabulary Loss

Words not only change their meanings, but are frequently discarded from the language. In the past, 'le-
man' meant 'sweetheart', 'regiment' meant 'government', and 'fond' meant 'foolish'. The following
words used in *Julius Caesar* are no longer current in
English but their meanings can usually be gauged
from the contexts in which they occur.

fain *(I, ii, 239)*: willingly, gladly
an *(I, ii, 262)*: if
rived *(I, iii, 6)*: split
thunderstone *(I, iii, 49)*: thunderbolt
ordinance *(I, iii, 66)*: natural order
factious *(I, iii, 118)*: active
spurn *(II, i, 11)*: strike, hit
exhalations *(II, i, 44)*: meteors
phantasma *(II, i, 65)*: nightmare
moe *(II, i, 72)*: more
palter *(II, i, 126)*: deceive
charactery *(II, i, 308)*: the things that are written
mortified *(II, i, 324)*: dead
ague *(II, ii, 113)*: severe fever

schedule *(III, i, 3)*: scroll
bayed *(III, i, 204)*: hunted until caught
marred *(III, ii, 194)*: mutilated
belike *(III, ii, 268)*: perhaps, it seems like
mart *(IV, iii, 11)*: market, bargain
vaunting *(IV, iii, 52)*: boasting
indirection *(IV, iii, 75)*: crooked deals
betimes *(IV, iii, 308)*: from time to time
proper *(V, iii, 96)*: own
is chanced *(V, iv, 32)*: turns out, happens
smatch *(V, v, 46)*: touch, small amount

Verbs

Shakespearean verb forms differ from modern usage in three main ways:

1. Questions and negatives could be formed without using 'do/did' as when Brutus asks:

What mean you? *(II, i, 234)*

where today we would say: 'What do you mean?' or when Portia instructs Lucius:

Stay not to answer me *(II, iii, 2)*

where modern usage demands: 'Do not stay to answer me'. Shakespeare had the option of using forms a. and b. whereas contemporary usage permits only the a. forms:

a.	b.
Do you know?	Know you?
Did you know?	Knew you?
I do not know	I know not
I did not know	I knew not.

2. A number of past participles and past tense forms are used which would be ungrammatical today. Among these are:

'took' for 'take':

> Where I have took them up *(II, i, 50);*

'untrod' for 'untrodden':

> Through the hazards of this untrod state *(III, i, 136);*

'strucken' for 'struck':

> How like a deer, strucken by many princes
> Dost thou lie here *(III, i, 209–210);*

'forgot' for 'forgotten':

> You have forgot the will I told you of *(III, ii, 236);*

and 'are rid' for 'have ridden':

> Brutus and Casius
> Are rid like madmen through the gates of Rome
> *(III, ii, 265–266).*

3. Archaic verb forms sometimes occur with 'thou' and with 'he/she/it':

> Shamest thou to show thy dangerous brows by
> night *(II, i, 78);*
> Thou hast some suit to Caesar *(II, iv, 27);*
> When the poor have cried, Caesar hath wept
> *(III, ii, 88).*

Pronouns

Shakespeare and his contemporaries had one extra pronoun 'thou' that could be used in addressing a person who was one's equal or social inferior. 'You' was obligatory when more than one person was addressed, as when Caesar told the conspirators:

> I could be well moved, if I were as you;
> If I could pray to move, prayers would move
>   me *(III, i, 58–59)*

but it could also be used to indicate respect, as when Antony recognizes the power of Octavius but reminds him:

> Octavius, I have seen more days than you *(IV, i, 18)*.

Frequently, a person in power used 'thou' to a child or a subordinate but was addressed 'you' in return, as when Portia speaks to Lucius:

> Portia: I prithee boy, run to the Senate House;
>   Stay not to answer me, but get thee gone.
>
> Lucius: Madam, what should I do?
>   Run to the Capitol, and nothing else?
>   And so return to you . . . *(II, iv, 1ff)*

but if 'thou' was used inappropriately it could cause grave offence as when, just before the assassination, Brutus addresses Caesar:

> I kiss thy hand, but not in flattery Caesar *(III, i, 52)*.

Prepositions

Prepositions were less standardized in Elizabethan English than they are today and so we find several uses in *Julius Caesar* that would have to be modified in contemporary speech. Among these are: 'on' for 'of' in:

> And be not jealous on me, gentle Brutus *(I, ii, 71)*;

'on' for 'at' in:

> If Caesar carelessly but nod on him *(I, ii, 118);*

'in' for 'from' in:

> There is no fear in him (i.e., There is nothing to
> fear from him) *(II, i, 190);*

'off' for 'down' in:

> How to cut off some charges in legacies *(IV, i,
> 9);*

and 'of' where today we would not require a preposition:

> And then I swore thee, saving of they life *(V, iii,
> 38).*

Multiple Negation

Contemporary English requires only one negative per statement and regards such utterances as "I haven't none" as nonstandard. Shakespeare often used two or more negatives for emphasis as when Brutus insisted:

> There is no harm intended to your person,
> Nor to no Roman else *(III, i, 90–91).*

POINT OF VIEW

Shakespeare's characters are too true-to-life to be pinned down in a phrase. They behave differently with different people, showing sides of themselves to friends that they hide from enemies. They have public selves and private selves. They are neither good nor evil, but a mixture of qualities. They are often inconsistent and unpredictable—gentle and considerate one moment, harsh and thoughtless the next. Don't ask Shakespeare to tell you what to think about them—he breathes life into his characters and lets them go. The rest is up to you.

FORM AND STRUCTURE

The play tells a single story that moves chronologically forward from (a) the plot against Caesar, to (b) the assassination, to (c) the results of the assassination (the retribution). The assassination takes place in Act III—the middle of the play; everything leads up to that moment, and away from it.

As in most Shakespeare plays, the action begins with the breakdown of order. Caesar has defeated the sons of Pompey, and the Senators are plotting against their ruler. The natural laws that bind a leader to his people have broken down. The divine plan has been shattered. The result is much like a sickness that infects everyone and everything—the conspirators, the people of Rome, the heavens themselves. At the end of the play, the Roman state is exhausted by war but on its way to recovery. The sickness has been controlled, and order reestablished.

Some say that *Julius Caesar* is a poorly structured play because the main character (Caesar) dies halfway through the play. Others argue that even though Caesar dies, his spirit dominates the entire play: it is Caesar's spirit that takes revenge on the conspirators; it is Caesar's spirit that lives on in the hearts of the people, and in the person of Octavius.

Caesar is well structured, even if you consider Brutus the main character, since the action begins with his involvement in the plot, and ends with his death and the eulogy over his body.

The Play

ACT I

ACT I, SCENE I

The opening scene (1) sets up the central conflict of the play, (2) introduces Caesar, and (3) introduces the citizens of Rome.

(1) THE CENTRAL CONFLICT

Something is amiss. The common people, who should be working, are in their holiday clothes and honoring the man who slaughtered the sons of Pompey. Two Roman officers, Flavius and Marullus, are rebelling against their ruler. Their reasons may or may not be just, but one thing is certain: the natural laws that bind a leader to his people have broken down. The order of the Roman state has been shattered.

The problem is not just political. In Shakespeare's world, life moves according to a divine plan; everyone has a set role to play, and a set relationship to each other. When someone or something disrupts this order it brings the whole structure down. Friend turns against friend. The very heavens are offended, and show their displeasure.

Marullus tells the Commoners to pray to the gods not to send a plague on them:

> Pray to the gods to intermit the plague
> That needs must light on this ingratitude.
> *Act I, Scene i, lines 57–58*

Behind Marullus' words is the belief that supernatural forces watch over us and pass judgment on our behavior. Throughout the play we'll see these forces at work, and learn what happens to people who deny their power.

(2) CAESAR

Caesar must be judged not only by what he says and does but by what others think of him. To the common people, he is a hero; to the two officers, he is a traitor to Rome.

Can we trust the judgment of the people? They seem neither to know nor to care about the man, and will accept anyone as their ruler, so long as he wins battles and gives them a day off from work.

Marullus and Flavius accuse Caesar of seeking unlimited power, but it is the power itself that seems to offend them rather than anything specific Caesar has done with it. No mention is made of Caesar depriving citizens of their civil liberties.

(3) THE CITIZENS OF ROME

Is Rome better off with a representative form of government or with a king? Is the assassination just or unjust? These are questions that cannot be answered without studying the needs and wishes of the common people of Rome. Collectively they are as important a "character" as Cassius, Brutus or Caesar.

If we can judge from the Cobbler (shoemaker), the Commoners like to pun and play. They are happy to have a holiday—whether to celebrate Caesar's return or Pompey's doesn't seem to matter much to them. They seem wrapped up in their own lives, less concerned with political issues than with having a day off from work. What interests the Cobbler, for instance, is the fact that people will be wearing out their shoes and bringing him business.

The people are easily manipulated. One moment they are gaily anticipating the festivities; the next, they are slinking away with shame. Says Marullus:

> See, whe'r their basest mettle be not moved;
> They vanish tongue-tied in their guiltiness.
>   *Act I, Scene i, lines 64–65*

This is the first of many times during the play when people are manipulated by the power of language—the power of words.

Do these people want or deserve a representative form of government? It doesn't seem so, for they lack the intelligence or interest to select rulers to represent them. What concerns them are the trappings of greatness—the pageantry and the glory. They will have their Caesar—whoever he may be. Julius Caesar will be murdered to give these people freedom; but from what we see of them in Scene i, it's questionable whether freedom is what they want or need.

ACT I, SCENE II

Lines 1–24

In the first scene we saw Caesar through the eyes of others. Now we see the man himself, and can judge him by his own words and actions.

Caesar orders his wife about, as a king orders his subjects:

> *Caesar.*   Calpurnia!
> *Calpurnia.* Here, my lord.
> *Caesar.* Stand you directly in Antonius' way.
> *Act I, Scene ii, lines 1–3*

Is Caesar wearing a public mask, or does he always greet his wife in such a cold and formal way?

Caesar tells Antony to touch his wife during the race, so that she can "shake off" the "curse" of sterility. The public Caesar may consider himself a god, but the private man is superstitious. And how tactless, announcing before the world that your wife is sterile! Calpurnia doesn't respond—but one wonders what she's thinking.

What is Antony's response to Caesar's request?

> When Caesar says "Do this," it is performed.
>> *Act I, Scene ii, line 10*

Anthony is either a flatterer, telling Caesar what he wants to hear, or he is genuinely devoted to Caesar, as a dog is to his master. In either case, Caesar clearly likes to give orders, and to be obeyed.

The Soothsayer now appears and warns Caesar to "Beware the ides of March." Caesar the private individual is obviously concerned, for he asks to see the man's face and have him repeat his message. But Caesar the public figure—in full view of his audience—refuses to acknowledge his fear, and dismisses the Soothsayer as a dreamer. There are thus two sides to Caesar—the private self and the legendary self he would like to become.

Lines 25–47

Brutus tells his friends that he will not go to the races. A man of conscience, he cannot play games while the Roman state is in turmoil. A man of principle, he values people for their inner worth, not for their physical strength. Life to him is not a competition with prizes to the swiftest.

Cassius complains like a child that Brutus doesn't love him anymore. Brutus reassures him. I neglect you, he says, only because I'm at war with myself.

Lines 48–89

Cassius now asks:

> Tell me, good Brutus, can you see your face?

And Brutus replies:

> No, Cassius; for the eye sees not itself
> But by reflection, by some other things.
>> *Act I, Scene ii, lines 51–53*

Because Brutus does not know himself, he must see himself reflected in others. His blindness to his own feelings is a tragic flaw that will eventually prove fatal. Like Caesar, he lets himself be mirrored in the eyes of others, and thus brings about his own destruction.

Cassius now goes to work on Brutus the way the serpent played on Eve. He calls Brutus good, noble, and gentle. He does not appeal to Brutus' ambition (Brutus has none), but points out that the most respected Romans are "groaning underneath this age's yoke."

Brutus now asks:

> Into what dangers would you lead me, Cassius,
> That you would have me seek into myself
> For that which is not in me?
> *Act I, Scene ii, lines 63-65*

Is Brutus deceiving himself to keep his hands clean? Does he really not know what Cassius has in mind? Is it true that conspiracy is not in his nature, or is he only trying to convince himself?

The crowds shout and Brutus admits his fear that "the people/Choose Caesar for their king." He is impatient with Cassius for keeping him so long, and for avoiding the issue. If what you have in mind is for the good of the people, he says, I will face death, if necessary, for

> I love
> The name of honor more than I fear death.
> *Act I, Scene ii, lines 88–89*

Brutus obviously means what he says, but isn't there something a bit suspect about someone who tells the world how virtuous he is?

Brutus is about to join a conspiracy and may simply want to reassure himself about the purity of his motives. Someone who knew himself, of course, would act from conviction, and not depend on the strength of his own words.

Lines 90–177

Cassius says that "Honor is the subject of my story," and then appeals to everything *but* honor. Carried away by jealousy and spite, he forgets that he is talking to Brutus, and uses arguments that would work only on himself. We were born free as Caesar, he says; "We both have fed as well, and we can both/ Endure the winter's cold as well as he." Such distinctions can mean nothing to a man as principled as Brutus.

Cassius discusses how he saved Caesar from drowning, and how Caesar once groaned and shook with fever. Brutus would never rate a person by his physical strength, but Cassius is too wrapped up in his private sense of injustice to notice or care.

Cassius' efforts to belittle Caesar say more about his own jealousy than about Caesar's right to rule. Cassius speaks of Caesar's "coward lips," but it is Caesar, not Cassius, who dared his friend to plunge into the Tiber on "a raw and gusty day." All Caesar can be accused of is a lack of physical stamina—which really has nothing to do with his strength as a ruler.

Like a child, Cassius cannot bear the injustice of a world in which he loses to his rival:

> And this man
> Is now become a god, and Cassius is
> A wretched creature, and must bend his body
> If Caesar carelessly but nod at him.
> *Act I, Scene ii, lines 115–118*

NOTE: On Womanly Behavior   Cassius accuses Caesar of behaving like "a sick girl," as if womanly behavior were an unpardonable sin. Yet in Shakespeare's world, men who deny their own feminine qualities—gentleness, mercy, and so on—are out of harmony with themselves and with the world.

Cassius blames himself for bowing to Caesar's will:

> The fault, dear Brutus, is not in our stars,
> But in ourselves, that we are underlings.
> *Act I, Scene ii, lines 140–141*

This is the sin of pride. Even Caesar knows at times that he is not the measure of all things, and bows to fate.

Just when we think we understand Cassius, he turns from spite to principle:

> Age, thou are shamed!
> Rome, thou hast lost the breed of noble bloods!
> When went there by an age, since the great
>   flood,
> But it was famed with more than one man?
> *Act I, Scene ii, lines 150–153*

It is a noble argument, but Cassius may just be trying to manipulate Brutus—playing on his friend's sense of family pride as the descendant of Lucius Junius Brutus, one of the founders of the Republic more than 400 years before.

There is no way of knowing what effect this appeal to family pride has on Brutus. True to his nature, he refuses to act impulsively, and keeps his feelings to himself. What we do know is family pride should not influence him—not if he is true to his principles.

As his talk with Brutus ends, Cassius says how glad he is to "have struck but thus much show/Of fire from Brutus" *(lines 176–177).*

NOTE: On Fire Imagery   "Fire" is an image you should follow closely throughout the play, for it represents the destructive powers of the universe, unleashed by the actions of Caesar, the common people, or the conspirators. Jump ahead for a moment to Casca's description of the storm in the opening lines of Act I, Scene iii:

> But never till tonight, never till now,
> Did I go through a tempest dropping fire.
> Either there is a civil strife in heaven,
> Or else the world, too saucy with the gods,
> Incenses them to send destruction.
> *Act I, Scene iii, lines 9–13*

Keep in mind this image of fire when you learn of Portia's unhappy fate, later in the play.

Lines 178–214

Caesar returns and describes Cassius as a dangerous man with "a lean and hungry look." This is such a delicious description that we're tempted to take it as the final word on Cassius. But Cassius has other, more admirable traits, which will become more evident after the assassination.

When Caesar speaks about Cassius *(lines 198–214),* notice the funny, almost pathetic way he switches roles from a private individual to a public figure:

The private Caesar is suspicious and fearful of Cassius. "Yond Cassius has a lean and hungry look," he says.

The public Caesar, of course, has to be above such human emotions as fear, and therefore announces for all the world to hear: "But I fear him not."

"Yet," says the private Caesar, "if my name were liable to fear,/I do not know the man I should avoid/So soon as that spare Cassius."

It is unthinkable for the great Caesar to be afraid, and so he puts his political mask back on and assures his audience: "I rather tell thee what is to be feared/ Than what I fear; for always I am Caesar."

If only he could be this legendary figure! But once again the mask slips, revealing an ordinary human being who is physically handicapped ("Come on my right hand, for this ear is deaf") and in need of reassurance ("And tell me truly what thou think'st of him.").

Is Caesar aware of the difference between the man and the mask? Does he deliberately fool his public to gain power (as any clever politician would do), or does he fool himself, too? There are no easy answers to these questions, but you will need to consider them before you can decide on Caesar's right to rule.

Antony tries to allay Caesar's fears about Cassius, and says:

> Fear him not, Caesar, he's not dangerous;
> *Act 1, Scene ii, line 196*

Could he be more wrong?

Lines 215–294

Caesar leaves with his followers, and Casca describes the events of the day—how Caesar three times refused the crown.

Was this a cynical gesture to manipulate the feelings of the public? It was Caesar's loyal follower Antony who offered the crown—perhaps the two politicians worked out their "act" beforehand. Casca thinks so, but Casca is one of the conspirators and would interpret events in a way that was unflattering to Caesar.

Casca is as cynical about the crowds as he is about
Caesar, and describes how

> the rabblement hooted, and clapped their chopt
> hands, and threw up their sweaty nightcaps, and
> uttered such a deal of stinking breath . . . that it
> had, almost, choked Caesar.
> *Act I, Scene ii, lines 243–247*

If Caesar "had stabbed their mothers," says Casca,
they still would have loved him *(lines 274–275).*

NOTE: On the Common People   If we can believe
Casca, the common people behaved collectively like a
blind beast, incapable of ruling itself or of knowing
what is in its own best interests.

Power in a republic comes ultimately from the people, who are supposed to have the wisdom to select
responsible leaders. The people of Rome seem to lack
this wisdom. Are they the true villains in *Julius Caesar*?
Is Shakespeare pointing out what happens to a country when the people ignore their responsibilities? Perhaps he is not passing judgment, but merely explor-
ing the historical reasons why Rome was transformed
from a republic into a monarchy.

Though Shakespeare may lack a democratic faith in
the common man, and be skeptical of the rabble's
right to self-rule, he is not necessarily as uncharitable
as Casca. Casca's harsh words remind us that most of
the conspirators are really fighting to retain their privileges, not to defend the rights of the people. On several occasions Caesar acts and speaks on behalf of his
public—something that cannot be said of his assassins.

Observe *(line 233)* that Brutus calls Casca "gentle." Throughout the play characters greet each other with similar terms of endearment which are either inappropriate or unfelt.

Observe, too, *(lines 284–286)* that Marullus and Flavius have been exiled or put to death. This is the only time in the play that Caesar deprives anyone of his civil liberties. Is this the act of a tyrant? Or is it the just verdict of a strong leader who refuses to tolerate treason?

Lines 295–322

Brutus calls Casca a dull-witted fellow. Cassius explains that Casca only pretends to be coarse and stupid so that people will listen to him. Cassius, the "great observer," understands such men, who use words to manipulate feelings, and pretend to be what they are not. Brutus, on the other hand, sees language as a way of expressing and communicating the truth, and is therefore easily fooled by people who use words as political weapons. How can he recognize irony when he is incapable of it himself? How can he recognize and deal with evil when he himself (some say) is such a noble man?

Cassius recognizes Brutus' dilemma:

> Well, Brutus, thou are noble; yet I see
> Thy honorable mettle may be wrought
> From that it is disposed; therefore it is meet
> That noble minds keep ever with their likes;
> For who so firm that cannot be seduced?
> *Act I, Scene ii, lines 308–312*

It is difficult to tell whether Cassius is delighted or saddened by his ability to "seduce" his noble friend— read the lines aloud and decide which interpretation seems more natural to you. In either case, Cassius comes across as a serpent seducing Innocence. If he succeeds, Innocence will be cursed for succumbing to an evil it does not understand. That may very well be the tragedy of Shakespeare's play.

ACT I, SCENE III

Lines 1–40

Casca describes some of the dreadful omens he has seen: the stormy seas; a lion (symbol of Caesar?) walking the streets; men on fire. The earth itself "Shakes like a thing unfirm" *(line 4)*.

Who is responsible for these strange happenings? Caesar—for overstepping the limits of his power? The conspirators—for plotting against him? The people—for allowing themselves to be manipulated against the best interests of the state?

All we know for certain is that evil has been set loose, and that it is affecting not just Rome but the entire universe. The disorder is like a sickness that started with a few individuals and now begins to spread until it infects everyone. Caesar, Brutus, and the other characters are not isolated human beings, acting in a vacuum; what each one does affects everyone else.

Cicero does not deny the importance of the omens, but points out that each person interprets them in his own way:

> Indeed, it is a strange-disposed time:
> But men may construe things after their fashion,
> Clean from the purpose of the things
>   themselves.
>
> *Act I, Scene iii, lines 33–35*

Lines 41–88

Other men are frightened by these supernatural happenings, but not Cassius. It has been "A very pleasing night to honest men," he says. Not only was he not afraid, he walked with his jacket unbuttoned, daring the heavens to strike him. Cassius shares Cicero's belief that the heavens are sending fearful warnings, but presumes to know that they are meant for Caesar, not for him. His cause, he feels, is noble—why should the gods punish him?

As arrogant as Caesar, Cassius forgets there may be forces in the world he can neither understand nor control. By opposing Caesar, whom he compares to the storm, Cassius feels he is opposing history, fate, the gods themselves. They, of course, will humble him in time.

Cassius, speaking to Casca, calls Caesar "A man no mightier than thyself, or me/In personal action" *(lines 76–77)*. Cassius thus weighs his worth against another man's—unlike Brutus, who weighs each person alone against absolute standards of right and wrong. Physical strength is what Cassius respects—unlike Brutus, who values people for their principles.

Cassius mourns the times he's living in, when Romans behave like women and meekly accept Caesar's rule:

> But woe the while! Our fathers' minds are dead
> And we are governed with our mothers' spirits;
> Our yoke and sufferance show us womanish.
> *Act I, Scene iii, lines 82–84*

Soft, feminine qualities frighten Cassius; he likes to see himself as the masculine ideal, who wins races and depends on nothing but his own courage and strength. Beneath this mask, however, lies the heart of a lost boy craving affection.

NOTE: On Cassius' Mother   Cassius' mother, we
discover later *(Act IV, Scene iii, lines 118–122)*, lacked
the same feminine qualities that Cassius fears to discover in himself. Did he have to prove his worth even
to her? If so, that might explain his competitive
nature, and his basic lack of confidence in his own
powers of judgment.

Lines 89–102

Cassius tells Casca he would rather kill himself than
live to see Caesar crowned. The human spirit can never be willingly enslaved, he says, because people are
always free to take our own lives. Cassius shows a
certain spirit of his own here, which makes it difficult
for us to dismiss him as a mere villian. Clearly, he
believes in the rightness of his cause, and is willing to
die for it. He may be foolish to ignore the gods, but
who is to say such foolishness is not the most noble
act of all?

Lines 103–164

Cassius believes the common people are as much to
blame as Caesar for turning him into a god:

> Poor man, I know he would not be a wolf
> But that he sees the Romans are but sheep;
>   *Act I, Scene iii, lines 104–105*

Cassius may simply wish to deny Caesar the credit for
his rise to power. But he is also pointing out what we
noted before, that the common people may be the real
villains for ignoring their responsibilities to the
Republic, and allowing it to fall.

ACT II

ACT II, SCENE I

Lines 1–34

The world admires Brutus as a man firm in his beliefs—a man who knows exactly who he is and what he wants. But the private man revealed here is so torn by doubts that he can hardly sleep.

Brutus has made up his mind: Caesar must die. "It must be by his death," he says—and then he searches for reasons to support his decision. How very human to choose a course of action, and then find reasons to support it!

Brutus' argument is based not on anything Caesar has done, but on what he *might* do. Is that sufficient grounds for murder? Cassius, at least, has real grievances against Caesar: The most respected men of Rome, he says, are "groaning underneath this age's yoke" *(Act I, Scene ii, line 61)*. Brutus, on the other hand, can speak only of what Caesar *might* become.

Further weakening Brutus' argument are these controversial lines:

> and, to speak the truth of Caesar,
> I have not known when his affections swayed
> More than his reason.
>> *Act II, Scene i, lines 19–21*

Is Brutus so shortsighted or so blind to human nature that he can't remember a single time when Caesar was swayed by his emotions?

NOTE: The Historic Caesar Shakespeare was familiar with historical records that portrayed Caesar's rule as a mixed blessing; why does Brutus ignore all of

Caesar's faults in his speech? Is Shakespeare trying to emphasize how flimsy Brutus' argument is, and how groundless his fears? Perhaps he also wants to show how dangerous logic is, when cut off from feeling.

Lines 35–60

Brutus is motivated not just by his principles but by a sense of family pride. His ancestor, Lucius Junius Brutus, helped drive the Tarquins from Rome and establish the Roman Republic. Brutus believes that for him to sit by and watch Caesar destroy the Republic would dishonor his family name.

It would be unfair to Brutus to say that he is motivated solely by a sense of pride. He is obviously deeply concerned about Caesar's threat to Roman institutions—just as we would be upset by a President, no matter how capable, who tried to undermine the power of the Senate. But pride plays a part in his decision—and thus his motives are less pure than he himself would like to believe.

Lines 61–68

Brutus blames Cassius for stirring him up against Caesar:

> Since Cassius first did whet me against Caesar,
> I have not slept.
>
> *Act II, Scene i, lines 61–62*

Is this true? Go back over the text—doesn't Brutus admit his fears of Caesar before he discusses them with Cassius? Brutus may be deluding himself to keep his conscience clean—blaming Cassius for what is essentially his own decision.

NOTE: On the Harmony of the World   Brutus compares the state of man to a "little kingdom." In Shakespeare's world nothing exists in isolation. The insurrection affects everything and everyone: the minds of the conspirators, Rome, the heavens themselves. The harmony of the individual mirrors the harmony of the state—which in turn mirrors the harmony of the universe. All are interrelated. When something happens to disturb this harmony, the whole structure comes tumbling down.

Lines 70–85

The conspirators enter, their faces buried in their cloaks, and Brutus is upset and embarrassed to associate with them. His conflict is one we all face at one time or another when we are forced to compromise ourselves (lie, cheat, etc.) for what we consider a greater good.

Lines 86–111

Cassius—who considers Brutus his good friend— immediately begins to play on Brutus' vanity:

> and no man here
> But honors you; and every one doth wish
> You had but that opinion of yourself
> Which every noble Roman bears of you.
> *Act II, Scene i, lines 90–93*

Brutus wants to know what cares are keeping his friends from sleep. Does he really not know? Can there by any question what these men are plotting? He may just be asking for details, or he may be trying once again to lay the blame for the plot on others in order to keep his own hands clean.

While Cassius confers with Brutus, the other conspirators—Casca, Cinna and Decius—debate where
the sun will rise. Dawn represents a new day, literally
and symbolically. Evil deeds, bad dreams, heavenly
disorders—these are associated with the night. Note
that the three conspirators can't agree on where the
sun will rise, and that Casca points toward the rising
sun with a sword.

Lines 112–140

In his speech to the conspirators, Brutus tries to
portray the assassination as a virtuous act. Taking an
oath, he argues, will put a stain on a noble enterprise.
To Brutus it is not a conspiracy, not a murder, but an
"enterprise." Like many public figures, he uses words
to cloak the horror of his deed.

Unlike Brutus, Cassius admits that the work at
hand is bloody, fiery, and terrible *(Act I, Scene iii, line
130)*. He too believes his goal is noble, but he is honest
with himself about the means he must use to accomplish his goal.

Is there such a thing as a virtuous murder? Can
good come from evil? Brutus hides from these questions, but his behavior forces us to ask them of ourselves.

Lines 141–161

Once Brutus joins the conspirators, he quickly takes
over. The others defer to his judgment. Metellus rec-
ommends that Cicero join them—his age will lend an
air of respectability to the plot. Brutus says no, "For he
will never follow anything/That other men begin."
This is Brutus' first decision as one of the conspirators;
is it a wise one? Cicero was Rome's greatest orator,
who might have swayed the crowds at Caesar's funeral, and changed the course of Roman history. Does
Brutus fear that Cicero will question his authority?

Notice how quickly Cassius accepts Brutus' judgment. Is the issue not important enough to risk a break with Brutus? Or does Cassius simply lack the confidence to stand up to his high-minded friend?

Brutus' second decision is to spare Antony's life. It is a decision that is morally correct, but politically disastrous. Trying to remain pure and faithful to his principles, he unleashes death and destruction on Rome, and dooms himself.

If Brutus had listened to Cassius and killed Antony, the conspirators might have restored power to the people and their elected representatives.

NOTE: Politics and Ideals   Does the world belong, then, to opportunists like Cassius—men or women with no consciences? Is Shakespeare suggesting that politics and ideals never mix? That a person with principles is doomed to failure in an imperfect world? These are chilling thoughts.

Lines 162–192

Brutus tries to elevate the murder into a religious sacrifice. "Let's be sacrificers, but not butchers," he says. "We shall be called purgers [healers], not murderers." He wants to carve Caesar

> as a dish fit for the gods,
> Not hew him as a carcass fit for hounds.
> *Act II, Scene i, lines 173–174*

Brutus is trying so hard not to compromise his principles! But is it possible? Isn't murder murder, whatever you call it? When a person lies dead, does it matter how the deed was done?

Of course, if the conspiracy is just and Caesar deserves to die, then the assassination is in fact a sacrifice of an individual for the sake of Rome. Brutus is to be admired for limiting the bloodshed, and for putting aside his own feelings for Caesar in order to do what he thinks is best for his country.

Brutus wishes he could kill the spirit of Caesar, but not the man. This is impossible, not just because the two are inseparable, but because the spirit, as we shall see, cannot be destroyed. The man can be killed, but what he represents is destined to live on.

Lines 193–233

Cassius and Decius portray Caesar as a man who is superstitious and easy to flatter. They see the man behind the mask, and question his ability to rule. What we must decide for ourselves is whether human frailty—which the general public never sees—is sufficient cause for insurrection.

The conspirators leave Brutus alone with the sleeping boy Lucius. Lucius seems to represent a world of childhood innocence to which Brutus wishes he could return.

The noble Brutus is by nature unfit for a political world of duplicity and intrigue. He would like to regain the inner harmony he has lost, but, for better or for worse, he has committed himself to political action, and there is no going back for him.

Brutus may be noble or foolish, but he has courageously decided to descend from his safe and privileged world of ideas and take a stand in a world of practical affairs.

Lines 233–325

Portia enters and we hear from her what we already know about Brutus: that he is introspective and torn by doubts; that he is a man of conscience who is struggling to do what is right. How different he is from those about him, who spend their time manipulating each other for private ends.

Brutus does not want to discuss the conspiracy with Portia; in fact, he lies to her, blaming his moodiness on ill health. Does he want to protect her from the ugly truth? Or is he simply too ashamed to own up to what he has done? In either case, he is less than honest, and we may condemn him for falling short of his standards, or praise him for giving in to the promptings of his heart.

Portia, with an intuitive wisdom, sees right through Brutus, and insists on the truth so that she can share his burden with him. He agrees to trust her with his secret, and she departs.

NOTE: Portia as a Modern Woman   Some people like to see Portia as a modern woman, hundreds of years ahead of her time. But is she really? She does refer to Brutus as her other half, and asks to be treated as his equal. Genuine respect and affection exist between them. She insists that she is stronger than other women—she is Cato's daughter, isn't she?—and should not be shielded from a world of men.

This image of herself, not as the woman "Portia," but as "Cato's daughter," is her public image of herself—the person she would like to become. (Brutus wears a mask, too, when he pictures himself as a descendant of a founder of the Roman Republic.)

Can Portia escape her private self and live up to her reputation as Cato's daughter? All we know to this point is that Brutus addresses her as "Portia," and that she greets him as "my lord." It is *his* world she seeks to enter—there is no question of Brutus entering hers. Equality seems to exist in terms of mutual respect within the framework of a traditional marriage, with pre-defined rights and obligations.

Lines 326–334

Brutus' dilemma—and one of the major issues of the play—is summed up in this brief dialogue:

> *Caius.*   What's to do?
> *Brutus.* A piece of work that will make sick men
>   whole.
> *Caius.* But are not some whole that we must
>   make sick?
> *Brutus.* That must we also.
> *Act II, Scene i, lines 326–329*

Brutus would rather focus on his noble end, and forget the means. Caius reminds him that people must suffer first. One can imagine the pain and resignation in Brutus' voice when he is forced to acknowledge that, yes, some must suffer before we can make the country healthy again.

Caius dos not wish to debate the issue—it is enough that Brutus leads him. Like Cassius and others, he defers to Brutus' judgment. It speaks well of Brutus that so many friends and associates are willing to follow him; and yet, are they any better than the common people who blindly follow Caesar? It seems in Shakespeare's play that whenever people give up responsibility for their lives and let themselves be led by others, the sickness of the state spreads and the world sinks further into a state of disorder.

ACT II, SCENE II

Lines 1–25

The scene opens in Caesar's home the morning of March 15th—the ides of March.

NOTE: On Omens   The thunder and lightning are stage effects which make the moment more dramatic. They also remind us that the order of the universe has been disturbed. The gods are unhappy with men and apparently will not rest until harmony has been restored.

Three times Calpurnia cried out in her sleep, "They murder Caesar!" Her dreams will soon come true— another indication that there are forces at work beyond our rational understanding or control. Some readers view Caesar's wife as a weak and frightened child, yet no one could be closer to the truth.

Shakespeare must have taken special delight in catching Caesar at his most private moment—in his dressing gown at home. If he ever intended to show the private man behind the public mask, now was the time.

He doesn't disappoint us. Caesar first appears as a frightened, superstitious man, asking for sacrifices to the gods. Calpurnia humiliates him by announcing, "You shall not stir out of your house today"; and Caesar immediately puts on his public mask, and says for all the world to hear:

> The things that threaten me
> Ne'er looked but on my back; when they shall see
> The face of Caesar, they are vanished.
> *Act II, Scene ii, lines 9–11*

Lines 26–54

Caesar would love to rise above normal human emotions, both to satisfy his own image of himself, and to satisfy his public. But the next moment he is his old superstitious self again, asking his servant what the augurers advise him to do. The fortune tellers caution him to stay home, but he is Caesar, isn't he?—more dangerous than danger itself.

Back and forth Caesar goes, from the private individual to the public figure: one moment succumbing to his private fears, the next, drawing back behind his mask, becoming the god he would like to be.

Is Caesar aware of the inconsistencies in his behavior? Possibly. But like many politicians, he may have worn his mask so often that, even in the privacy of his home, he can no longer tell when it is on or off.

Lines 55–68

Caesar finally gives in to his wife's wishes and agrees to stay home. Perhaps he is being a considerate and loving husband; it is more likely, however, that he is using her as an excuse to hide his own fears from himself and from the public.

Worried that his concession to her may be taken for weakness, he tries to act like the mighty emperor again, and announces to Decius, "I will not come today."

That Caesar's concerned about his public image is obvious. What is less certain is whether he is blindly obsessed with it, or simply shrewd enough to recognize the need to project a strong public image.

Lines 69–106

Shakespeare's characters, from a simple cobbler to a noble senator, are continuously being manipulated by others—and Caesar is no exception. To convince him to visit the Senate, Decius first plays upon his vanity—interpreting Calpurnia's dream as "a vision fair and fortunate" of Romans bathing in Caesar's blood to restore their health. Next, he plays upon Caesar's ambition, telling him the Senate plans this very day to offer him the crown. Will the great Caesar have the Senators whispering that he is afraid?

Caesar is an actor who comes alive in the eyes of his audience, and nothing could upset him more than the loss of his public's esteem. To be afraid is to be merely mortal, and Caesar wants to cast himself in the role of a god. And so he laughs at Calpurnia's fears—fears he shared only a moment ago—and goes to the Senate, and to his death.

Lines 107–129

Caesar is strikingly polite to his would-be assassins—thanking them for their "pains and courtesy," blaming himself for keeping others waiting, and inviting them to share some wine with him.

This is a side of Caesar's nature that we have not seen before. Is Shakespeare painting him in a favorable light to emphasize the horror of the assassination? Perhaps he is merely showing how doublefaced politicians can be in public.

ACT II, SCENE III

Artemidorus' note gives Caesar another chance to save his life—will he read it? The possibility of a reprieve stretches out the time before Caesar meets his fate, and therefore adds to the suspense.

Artemidorus considers Caesar a friend, and is willing to risk his life for him. How sad it is, he says, that virtuous men like Caesar cannot live beyond the reach of jealous rivals:

> My heart laments that virtue cannot live
> Out of the teeth of emulation.
>> *Act II, Scene iii, lines 12–13*

How different a view of Caesar from that of the conspirators! Could both be right? Shakespeare makes us realize that there is no final verdict on a human being—that a friend to one person may be an enemy to another, and that our opinions say as much about ourselves as they say about others.

ACT II, SCENE IV

Shakespeare again delays the assassination attempt, and thereby adds to the suspense.

Brutus, true to his word, has shared his secret with Portia, and she is having trouble keeping it to herself.

The elements in Portia, as in Brutus, are at war: "I have a man's mind," she says, "but a woman's might." In this disordered world there is no harmony anywhere: neither in the heavens, nor in the heart and mind of a noble woman.

Portia is almost mad with fear. She would like to be "Cato's daughter," but she is only "Portia," and must admit:

> Ay me, how weak a thing
> The heart of woman is!
> *Act II, Scene iv, lines 39–40*

Like Brutus and Caesar, Portia tries to live up to her name and brings about her own destruction.

ACT III

ACT III, SCENE I

It's March 15th, the ides of March. Will the soothsayer's prophecy come true? The play has been building towards this dramatic moment when Caesar confronts his fate.

Lines 1–12

The scene begins before the Capitol, where Caesar refuses to accept a note warning him about the plot. "What touches us ourself shall be last served," he says.

What do you think: are these the words of a shrewd and deceitful politician who puts on airs of false humility to impress the crowds? Or does Caesar see himself as the servant of the people? The question is the same you already asked about Caesar's motives when he refused three times to accept the crown (*Act I, Scene ii, lines 234–250*). Whatever your interpretation, it's ironic that, had Caesar acted *more* selfishly, he might have saved his life.

Lines 13–75

The conspirators now have Caesar alone, and petition him to grant a reprieve to Metallus' banished brother, Publius Cimber. Why they choose this moment is open to interpretation. It may be merely an excuse to get Caesar alone. Perhaps they know that Caesar's almost certain refusal will harden their hearts, and sharpen their resolve to kill him. Perhaps, too, they are offering Caesar a final chance to redeem himself through an act of mercy. It's fun to speculate what the conspirators would have done if Caesar had relented.

Caesar now makes two speeches that give important clues to his character. Read these passages carefully, for they give you a rare opportunity to decide just how fit he is to rule.

In his first speech (*lines 35–48*), Caesar lashes out at Metellus for trying to sway him (Caesar) with flattery. Caesar has a point: it's not very flattering—it's downright insulting—to be told how great you are by someone who is obviously trying to manipulate your feelings. Perhaps it's the implication that Caesar can't see through someone as unsubtle as Metellus that annoys Caesar most.

NOTE: Two Views of Caesar   Some readers argue that Caesar's refusal to submit to flattery or to the pleadings of friends shows that he is a strong ruler with the courage of his convictions. Without such a strong captain at the helm, these readers argue, the Roman ship would flounder.

Other readers disagree. Caesar's inflexibility shows that he is callous and arrogant, they argue—a tyrant afraid to change his mind for fear of appearing weak before his friends.

In his second speech, Caesar compares himself to the Northern Star,

> Of whose true-fixed and resting quality
> There is no a fellow in the firmament.
> *Act III, Scene i, lines 61–62*

To call himself the only Roman who remains constant in his beliefs seems outrageous enough—but Caesar goes beyond this. I make my own destiny, he seems to be saying; I am stronger than fate. Like a god, I am free from the ravages of old age, sickness, and death.

Some readers see this speech as the sad ravings of an aging man who has lost all grasp of reality. Others view it as a carefully developed political speech meant to reinforce his public image as a monarch. In either case, Caesar is guilty of arrogance and blasphemy against the gods.

However you interpret Caesar's words, they do give the conspirators the excuse they need to murder him; and so, in some sense, Caesar's pride is responsible for his own downfall. Whether this pride is in itself sufficient justification for murdering him is something you'll have to decide for yourself. Your verdict will depend in part on whether you judge Caesar (and people in general) by what he is or by what he does.

Lines 76–77

It does speak well for Caesar that at the moment of death he seems most upset by the betrayal of Brutus. If you, my closest friend, could betray me—Caesar seems to be saying—then let me die.

As death approaches, the mask slips, and the man beneath reveals himself. What upsets Caesar most is not the loss of glory, or even death itself—but the disloyalty of a friend. Perhaps at this final moment Caesar realizes the truth about himself. If that's the case, then we have to pity him for learning the truth too late.

Lines 78–97

The conspirators reveal themselves in the different ways they react to Caesar's death. Cassius and his followers are political men who recognize the need to deal with the crowds. While Brutus, the idealist, stands about philosophizing about fate, the others rush about, trying to cope with the public outcry. Brutus seems to believe that he lives in a moral universe in which good must triumph over evil. He believes that people are as rational as he is, and will understand the justice of his cause. Cassius, the realist, recognizes the need to manipulate the emotions of the people. Rather than wait for virtue to triumph, he takes matters into his own hands.

Lines 98–118

Casca observes that people live in fear of death. Then we are Caesar's friends, says Brutus, for we have shortened the time he had to live in fear:

> So are we Caesar's friends, that have abridged
> His time of fearing death.
> *Act III, Scene i, lines 104–105*

Having murdered Caesar, Brutus now convinces himself that he has done the man a favor! So strong is the power of words, and so dangerous is logic when cut off from genuine feeling, that they can transform butchery into a noble act.

Lines 119-121

As the conspirators prepare to depart, Cassius remarks:

> Brutus shall lead, and we will grace his heels
> *Act III, Scene i, line 120*

Now that Cassius has enlisted Brutus' support, he seems ready to let Brutus take charge. Does he lack confidence in his own judgment? Or is he simply not motivated by personal ambition? In either case, it's interesting to note that Cassius, who refused to stoop to Caesar's will, seems happy to give in to Brutus'.

Lines 122–163

Antony would like to meet with Brutus to learn why Caesar was killed. If Brutus can justify his actions, Antony agrees to follow him as once he followed Caesar. Brutus, always willing to explain the justice of his cause, happily consents.

Antony's devotion to Caesar blinds him to Caesar's faults—as Cassius' hatred of Caesar blinds him to Caesar's virtues. Yet, when Antony addresses the conspirators, he shows himself to be an independent thinker with a deep understanding of human nature. If he had simply announced that he was switching sides, the conspirators would probably not have believed him—they would have questioned his motives. His outpouring of grief over Caesar's death offends them, but it makes them trust him, because he seems honest and sincere.

NOTE: Antony, A Sincere Opportunist   A cynical opportunist—that's how most people describe Antony. Yet he always speaks with deep conviction. His motives are always suspect, and yet—unlike any of the other men—he seems to remain faithful to his feelings. Is it possible to be an opportunist, then, and also a person who speaks from the heart?

Lines 164–223

You can see the basic difference between Brutus and Cassius in the way they respond to Antony.

Brutus appeals to Antony's intellect with the argument that "pity to the general wrong of /Rome . . . Hath done this deed on Caesar" *(lines 170, 172)*. Is this any way to win the heart of Caesar's most devoted friend? Brutus' problem is not so much that he ignores human nature, as that he assumes others have natures like his own. Whether his words to Antony reveal a man who is cold and unfeeling, or simply too pure and noble for this world, is something you'll have to decide for yourself. Either way, he's the direct opposite of Antony.

As Brutus appeals to Antony's "higher" instincts, so Cassius appeals to his "lower"—offering him a share of political power. This is the sort of appeal that would work on Cassius himself.

When Brutus promises to justify the assassination, Antony responds, "I doubt not of your wisdom" *(line 184)*. What he is saying to himself is, yes, you are wise and have your reasons, but none of them can make the deed less terrible.

Lines 225–226

Brutus believes his reasons are so strong

> That were you, Antony, the son of Caesar,
> You should be satisfied.
> *Act III, Scene i, lines 225–226*

Could reason or logic ever be strong enough to make a person applaud the murder of his father? Brutus thinks so, and in that belief lies his weakness— and his strength.

Lines 227–253

Brutus decides over Cassius' objections to let Antony speak at Caesar's funeral. The decision is admirable, but politically disastrous.

Brutus plans to speak first, "And show the reason of our Caesar's death" *(line 237)*. What he fails to understand is that most people are not convinced by *reasons*. What motivates them are appeals to their emotions. (Brutus would never admit it, but he himself was led by his feelings when he joined the conspiracy to live up to his family name.)

Lines 254–275

Left alone, Antony reveals his true intentions. What we discover is a man of genuine passion, overcome by feelings he can neither completely understand nor control. As Brutus responds with his head, so Antony reacts with his heart. He has no concern about the future or about the best interests of Rome. Values, ideals, principles—these mean nothing to him. He cannot see beyond the murder of a friend and his desire for revenge.

Antony becomes the servant of Caesar's vengeful spirit—serving him in death as he served him in life. His devotion is total and blinds him to everything else—even the "blood and destruction" he is about to unleash on guilty and innocent alike. Whether he is an instrument of good or evil depends, of course, on how you view the man he serves.

One thing that can't be doubted is the sincerity of Antony's feelings. In a world of men too circumspect to speak their minds, it comes as a relief to find one who can express himself with tears.

Lines 276–297

The scene ends with the convenient arrival of Octavius' servant, who announces that Octavius and his men are camped about 21 miles from Rome. Caesar, apparently sensing danger, had written Octavius for his support. Let him stay there, says Antony, until I have made my speech and determined whether the time is ripe for his return.

ACT III, SCENE II

The two funeral orations should be studied for what they say about (1) Brutus, (2) Antony, (3) Caesar, and (4) the crowds.

Brutus and Antony

You can argue—though not many people do—that Brutus' speech is as powerful and convincing as Anto-

ny's, and that it fails only because Antony has the
final word. Defenders of Brutus' speech point out
that:

- He flatters the common people by treating them
as equals and appealing to their powers of reason.
- He involves the people by asking them questions.
- His questions are rhetorical; their answers are
self-evident. (The answer to the question, "Who is
here so base, that would be a bondman [slave]?" is, of
course, "No one.") The rhetorical question is used by
public speakers to make audiences think they are
reaching their own decisions, when in fact their
minds are being made up for them.
- He plays upon the sympathy of his audience—
offering to sacrifice himself for his country.
- His speech is brief and to the point.
- He does convince his audience. When he finishes
speaking, the citizens exclaim, "This Caesar was a
tyrant," and "We are blest that Rome is rid of
him."

Other readers argue that Brutus' speech is weaker
than Antony's. They point out that:

- Brutus appeals to the minds of the people; Antony sways them by tugging at their emotions.
- Brutus appeals to an abstract sense of duty to the
state; Antony appeals to greed.
- Brutus asks the people to appreciate degrees of
good and evil; Antony plays upon their need to love
and hate.
- Brutus begins his speech by addressing the people *collectively* as Romans; Antony addresses them
individually as friends. Antony knows instinctively
that personal relationships mean more to people than
their identification with the state.

• Brutus speaks in prose, which appeals to the intellect; Antony speaks in verse, which appeals to the emotions. Brutus' speech is not strong or important enough to be dignified with verse.

• Brutus makes the politically disastrous mistake of expecting too much from the people. He reasons with them as though they were his intellectual equals. He uses language, not to manipulate feelings, but to communicate ideas. He throws out concepts with balance, precision and speed.

> As Caesar loved me, I weep for him; as he was fortunate, I rejoice at it; as he was valiant, I honor him; but, as he was ambitious, I slew him. There is tears, for his love; joy, for his fortune; honor, for his valor; and death, for his ambition.
>
> *Act III, Scene ii, Lines 24–29*

This verbal juggling act may impress Brutus' educated friends, but who can believe that it moves the hearts of the people? Heroes and villains are what they want—black-and-white distinctions, not shades of gray.

Antony's speech may not be as concise or intellectually clever, but it appeals to people on a level that they can understand. Avoiding fine distinctions, he portrays Caesar as a hero who was betrayed by friends:

> . . Brutus, as you know, was Caesar's angel.
> Judge, O you gods, how dearly Caesar loved
>   him!
> That was the most unkindest cut of all;
> For when the noble Caesar saw him stab,
> Ingratitude, more strong than traitors' arms,
> Quite vanquished him.
>
> *Act III, Scene ii, lines 183–188*

This is language the people can relate to, for who has not been stung by the ingratitude of a friend?

• Brutus speaks as though his words were memorized—he could be addressing anyone. Antony seems to form his words as he goes along, in response to the shifting moods of his audience. His speech, therefore, seems more spontaneous, and more deeply felt.

• Brutus projects an image of complete self-control when he speaks; Antony pretends to break down and cry. The people listen to Brutus with respect, but he is an intellectual, and they do not identify with him. Antony is as passionate as the people, and they consider him one of their own.

• Brutus reaches the people only through their minds; Antony touches them through their senses as well, showing them Caesar's body and Caesar's bloody cloak—the same one he wore in one of his most decisive military victories. Antony wins their admiration by repeating that the assassins are all honorable men, and pretending that he is just an ordinary fellow who has no grudge to bear.

• The failure of Brutus' speech is summed up in the words of the Third Plebeian: "Let him [Brutus] be Caesar." No intellectual argument is going to reduce the needs of the people for Caesar, and for what he represents. If Caesar the man is dead, they will find someone to take his place.

• Antony may be a cynical opportunist, stopping at nothing to get what he wants. And yet he also seems to believe what he says, and to speak from the heart. He does appeal to the so-called baser instincts of his audience, but only to accomplish what he considers a noble end. Ambition is apparently not his motive: revenge is what he seeks—revenge for the death of a dear friend. Is revenge a motive less honorable than jealousy (Cassius) or the wish to right wrongs that have not yet been committed (Brutus)?

Caesar

Caesar manages to surprise us even after his death.
According to Antony, Caesar leaves the people his
parks, his gardens, and a sum of money. Would a
tyrant be so generous? Caesar may simply have tried
to buy himself immortality—to win in death the uni-
versal respect and admiration he was unable to attain
in life. But whatever his motives he was interested in
the well-being of his public. Would Brutus and the
other conspirators have been as generous?

The Crowds

The crowd's reaction to the two speeches suggests
that the common people are incapable of ruling themselves. What they seem to need is a strong, benevolent authority figure—someone to give order and
direction to their blind impulses. If Caesar is killed,
they will keep his spirit alive in Brutus, Antony, or
someone else.

Brutus assumes that all Romans are noble, but
Rome is not just an ideal, it is also a community of
people. Like Brutus himself, Rome has both a public
and a private face. The Rome which Brutus appeals to
is peopled with wise and virtuous citizens who zeal-
ously guard their freedom. The actual people, however, are greedy, fun-loving and thoughtless—happy to
sign over their freedom to anyone who struts about
like a hero and promises them a day off from work.
They can also be vicious, as we shall see in the following scene.

Shakespeare's portrait of the common people is not
very flattering. The reason may simply be that Shakespeare lived in a pre-democratic age. Yet ask yourself:
are people today more capable of self-government
than they were in Roman times?

ACT III, SCENE III

The poet Cinna is murdered by an angry mob because he has the same name as one of the conspirators. Why is a poet the crowd's first victim? Perhaps because the murder of someone so obviously innocent and apolitical emphasizes the horror of the deed. Perhaps Shakespeare is suggesting—though he does not actually say so—that artists have no place in a world torn by civil strife, since it is the artist's job to create order from disorder, and to insist upon the truth.

The murder reminds us how dangerous the masses are when their emotions are unchecked. It also foreshadows months of death and destruction, to innocent and guilty alike.

NOTE: On the Power of Names   Cinna the poet is murdered because he has the same name as one of the conspirators. How powerful names are, and how often people mistake them for the person beneath! Portia, Brutus, Caesar—all try to live up to their names and bring about their own destruction. The crowds are happy to call Brutus "Caesar," because it is the name that matters to them, not the man.

ACT IV

ACT IV, SCENE I

The "dogs of war" have been set loose. The sickness that began with Caesar's death has spread and infected the entire state of Rome. In a world without order, brother kills brother and friend kills friend.

Antony checks off the names of men to die as casually as someone checking off items on a shopping list. This is clearly not the "freedom" Brutus envisioned for the people of Rome after the death of Caesar.

Antony is ruthless. He is a man without conscience, who will let nothing—not honor, not friendship—stand in his way. Yet he remains a devoted friend to Caesar. He is also honest with himself and does not try to be something he is not. He is brutally effective. He is a realist who is will- ing to dirty his hands to achieve what he considers noble ends.

Antony plans to deprive the people of the money promised them in Caesar's will. A contemptible act, yes, yet necessary perhaps to raise an army to fight the conspirators.

Antony makes use of Lepidus, then scoffs at him behind his back—refusing to share power with such a "barren-spirited fellow" who feeds on the fashions of the moment.

Antony reveals himself both in his willingness to manipulate and kill and in his readiness to defy even Caesar's wishes for the people. He is wonderfully clearsighted and self-controlled, and yet obsessed by the desire for revenge. His mission defines him; it gives him a purpose in life without which, it seems, he cannot exist.

ACT IV, SCENE II

The betrayal of a friend disturbs the harmony of the universe and brings death and destruction to Rome. In this disordered world, relationships are poisoned by distrust. People know as little about each other as they know about themselves.

The disintegration of the Republic continues. Rome is split into two warring factions, and the members of the factions are quarreling among themselves.

Brutus is angry at Cassius, but rather than give in to his emotions, he makes a speech about the nature of love. When love begins to cool we put on a formal show of affection, he says; true love needs no such formalities to support it. How like Brutus to turn his own emotions into a general theory of human nature.

His feelings under control as usual, Brutus points out the need for him and Cassius to put on a show of affection before their troops, and to air their grievances in private. Is this a new Brutus—advocating deceit? It is strange to see Brutus acting more pragmatically than Cassius. Brutus may be a man of ideas, but he is also a man with a practical knowledge of the world.

ACT IV, SCENE III

Your reaction to the quarrel between Cassius and Brutus will say as much about you as it says about them. If you are the sort of person who compromises his values to get what he wants, you will probably sympathize with Cassius. If you are a person who sticks to his principles at all costs, you will probably sympathize with Brutus. Many readers find their sympathies shifting at this point in the play to Cassius, since Brutus treats him coldly, and Cassius tries so hard to remain friends.

Lines 1–27

Cassius feels wronged because Brutus has ignored his letter seeking pardon for his friend Lucius Pella. Brutus has disregarded Cassius' plea and publicly disgraced Pella for taking bribes. In times like these, says Cassius, we can't afford to pay attention to such minor crimes.

Brutus, in turn, scolds Cassius for being no better than Pella—selling positions to men who don't deserve them. Let's not debase ourselves by taking bribes, says Brutus; we killed Caesar because he abused his power—his death was pointless if we stoop to the same crimes.

Brutus thus refuses to compromise his principles. Should we admire him for being so steadfast? Or criticize him for being inflexible and not consulting with Cassius before disgracing Pella? Accepting bribes in times of war seems trivial—not important enough to risk dissension between the two top generals. Brutus may be high-minded, but at times like this he also seems smug and self-righteous.

Lines 28–68

What begins as a discussion between two grown men soon becomes a kids' squabble:

> *Brutus.* You are not, Cassius.
> *Cassius.* I am.
> *Brutus.* I say you are not.
> > *Act IV, Scene iii, lines 33–34*

> *Brutus.* Peace, peace, you durst not so have
>   tempted him [Caesar].
> *Cassius.* I durst not?
> *Brutus.* No.
> *Cassius.* What? Durst not tempt him?
> *Brutus.* For your life your durst not.
> > *Act IV, Scene iii, lines 59–62*

By this point, there are no principles at stake—only pride. Brutus, the man of high moral standards, steps out from behind his mask of stoic resignation, and what does he do? He baits, threatens, and insults his friend. Is this the "real" Brutus, at last?

Brutus now retreats again behind high-minded phrases. Wearing his words like armor he says:

> There is no terror, Cassius, in your threats;
> For I am armed so strong in honesty
> That they pass me by as the idle wind
> *Act IV, Scene iii, lines 66–68*

Brutus *is* honest, yet there is something offensive about his boasting about it. Would he need to, if he believed it himself? He seems as sure of himself as Caesar, when Caesar compared himself to the Northern Star, moments before his death.

Lines 69–121

Brutus is also angry with Cassius for failing to send money to pay for his troops. "I did send to you/For certain sums of gold, which you denied me," he complains; "For I can raise no money by vile means." *(lines 69–71).*

Brutus can be admired for his principles. He can also be condemned as a hypocrite, who is perfectly happy to take money from the peasants, so long as Cassius does the dirty work and lets him (Brutus) keep his own hands clean.

Cassius insists that he did not deny Brutus funds; that his messenger "was but a fool/That brought my answer back." Is he telling the truth? Whether he is or not, Brutus might have checked with Cassius before accusing him of withholding funds.

Brutus seems to care more about his lofty principles than about friendship. Cassius cares passionately about friendship, and says, convincingly:

> A friend should bear his friend's infirmities;
> But Brutus makes mine greater than they are.
> *Act IV, Scene iii, lines 85–86*

What has gotten into Brutus—what has made him lose his perspective and his self-control? Behind the mask apparently is a man no different from the rest of us: a collection of drives and passions, painted over with a thin layer of thought.

Note *(lines 118–122)* that Cassius blames his mother for giving him a quick temper ("rash humor"). Was his mother unloving? That might explain Cassius' craving for affection.

Lines 122–141

A Poet now enters and speaks perhaps for Shakespeare when he says, "Love, and be friends" *(line 130)*. It is the absence of love and friendship that has plunged Rome into civil war, and inflamed the heavens. The Poet appears like a Biblical prophet, bearing the truth—"Love, and be friends"—and no one hears or cares to listen. The Poet, unlike Cinna, escapes with his life, but neither can be heard above the sounds of war. As Brutus himself says,

> What should the wars do with these jigging
> [rhyming] fools?
>
> *Act IV, Scene iii, line 136*

NOTE: The Voice of Shakespeare Himself   The poet may indeed be a fool, with no sense of time and place; but he may also speak for Shakespeare, reminding us that artists have a responsibility to share their vision with us, just as we have a responsibility to listen.

The foolishness perhaps is not in the Poet's simply rhymes, but in Brutus' rude and hasty response:

> Get you hence, sirrah! saucy fellow, hence!
> *Act IV, Scene iii, line 133*

Even Cassius is more charitable, and says:

> Bear with him, Brutus, 'tis his fashion.
> *Act IV, Scene iii, line 134*

Lines 142–160

The Poet leaves, and Brutus announces that his wife, Portia, has killed herself. Throughout his quarrel with Cassius, he kept the news to himself. He reveals the truth in such a cold, abrupt manner that we are left wondering if this is a man incapable of love. And yet the fact that Brutus can control his emotions may indicate a strong self-will rather than an absence of feeling. To accept calmly whatever fate brings is a basic principle of his Stoic philosophy. To refuse to burden others with his grief is in keeping with his noble nature. Perhaps he realizes that a sorrow as great as his cannot be shared, and that any effort to reduce it to words can only cheapen it. If there is genuine grief behind Brutus' silence, then his childlike behavior with Cassius suddenly becomes clear. What we have witnessed is the anger and frustration of a man nursing a hidden sorrow.

Note that Portia *(lines 151–155)* kills herself by swallowing fire [hot coals]. It is an appropriate way for her to die, since fire is a symbol of the destructive powers of the gods, unleashed (some say) by the actions of her husband Brutus.

Lines 161–194

Messala arrives with letters reporting that Octavius and Antony have put to death from seventy to one hundred senators, including Cicero. The common people, then, are not the only ones who need their emotions held in check!

NOTE: **Two Versions of the Play**   Brutus tells
Messala that he has not heard of Portia's death,
although just a moment ago Brutus was announcing
her death to Cassius. It's possible that Brutus is
putting on an act for Messala, using the opportunity
to reinforce his public image as a Stoic. Cassius, realizing this, may have played along. Most critics
believe, however, that Shakespeare later revised the
scene, and that either he, his editor, or his printer
forgot to delete one of the two passages relating the
news of Portia's death.

The second passage—the one in which Brutus
learns the news from Messala—is much less flattering
to Brutus, because of the almost inhuman speed with
which he dismisses his wife's death and moves on to
the subject of war. "Why, farewell, Portia," he says;
and then after a few high-minded words on the inev-
itability of death, he adds, "Well, to our work alive.
What do you think/Of marching to Philippi present-
ly?" *(lines 189–196)*. It is generally believed that Shakespeare wrote this version first, which emphasizes Brutus' stoicism; and that he deleted it and added the
earlier passage *(lines 141–158)*, which emphasizes Brutus' humanity.

Lines 195–228

Brutus and Cassius now discuss strategy: whether
to keep their position on the heights and wait for the
enemy to attack, or to take the offensive and try to
catch the enemy off guard.

Although Brutus asks Cassius what he thinks, his
mind is already made up. In his military strategy, as in
his philosophy, he is convinced that he is right and

has no patience for compromise or debate. What could be more tactless than his response to Cassius:

> Good reasons must of force give place to better.
> *Act IV, Scene iii, line 202*

When Cassius politely asks to be heard—"Hear me, good brother," he says—Brutus ignores him and makes one of his high-minded speeches about the need to act when the time is ripe *(lines 215–223)*. Cassius realizes that it is useless to argue with someone so obstinate, and bows to Brutus' stronger will.

Brutus does not hesitate to make difficult military decisions, so it is unfair to call him a man of ideas, incapable of action. And yet it is perhaps the newness of his job, and his desire to prove himself worthy of it, that make him seek a single, decisive victory.

Lines 229–307

Brutus, having broken his silence about Portia, seems able to relax again, if only for a moment. He asks Lucius—symbol of youth and innocence—to play music, perhaps so that he can hear the harmonies of a simpler, more carefree time. He puts his own concerns aside and considers the comforts of his men. When Lucius falls asleep, he is too considerate to wake him up.

Lucius has no guilty conscience to interrupt his sleep. Brutus, however, is kept awake by Caesar's ghost, who promises to reappear at the decisive battle at Philippi.

NOTE: The Ghost of Caesar   The ghost is a reminder that there are powers in the world that control our fate—powers that cannot be grasped by logic and reason. The ghost is also a dramatic way of portraying an image in a nightmare—an image that embodies the guilt and self-doubt beneath Brutus' firm exterior.

The ghost vanishes and Brutus wakens his men. Lucius, not realizing that he has fallen asleep, worries that his instrument is out of tune. "The strings, my lord, are false" *(line 290),* he says.

And so they are. The harmonies of life have been drowned out by the cries of men in their sleep and by the baying of "the dogs of war." Musicians, like poets, won't be heard again until order is restored, and the Roman state is back on its heaven-appointed course.

ACT V

ACT V, SCENE I

Shakespeare has structured his play around the assassination and the consequences of the assassination. By the final act the issues have all been spelled out; events now take their course, and fate has its way. As Brutus says, "This same day/Must end that work the ides of March begun" *(lines 112-113).*

NOTE: A Struggle For Power   Brutus joined the conspiracy because of his love for Rome, yet he never speaks of what the senators might do with their newly-restored powers, nor does he envision a better world without Caesar. The silence of both factions on all issues beyond the current battle suggests that they are engaged primarily in a power struggle over two forms of government—a monarchy and a republic. Both factions say they care about the people, but both manipulate the people for private ends.

Brutus and Cassius seem gripped by a sense of doom. They go through the motions of fighting, but seem to understand intuitively that fate has already decided against them. All that is left for them is to play their parts as nobly as they can.

Lines 1–20

Brutus' decision to abandon the heights was not wise; even Antony did not believe Brutus would be foolish enough to give up his strategic advantage. Antony orders Octavius to lead his troops along the left side of the battlefield. Octavius refuses, not for any military reasons, it seems, but because "I will do so." Octavius behaves as willfully as a young Caesar who needs to remind others of his power. Antony bows to Octavius, perhaps because he knows the issue is not important enough to fight about, or because he recognizes Octavius' right to rule.

Lines 21–68

The four generals meet on the plains of Philippi and battle each other with words. Antony, Cassius and Brutus take turns trying to deflate each other's egos. Brutus takes particular delight in this verbal swordplay. Only Octavius keeps his perspective, urging them to get to the business at hand.

Lines 69–125

Cassius, sensing that he is about to die, wants the world to know that he is following Brutus' battle plan against his will. Two sides of Cassius are apparent here. His need to prove himself a man shows in his concern for his reputation as a soldier; and his craving for affection shows in his willingness to die rather than oppose the wishes of his good friend Brutus.

NOTE: The Importance of Omens   Cassius now believes in omens—in forces beyond his rational understanding and control. He used to think the gods were indifferent to men, but now acknowledges the existence of supernatural forces that shape his destiny. What he has learned is that people can't control their fate, yet are held accountable for their actions, and are ultimately rewarded or punished for everything they do.

How different Brutus and Cassius behave when they are alone together, and can put aside their threats and boasts, and be themselves. Because danger and doom press down upon them, they are more honest than ever before. Cassius asks the gods for victory, not so that he can gain riches and power, but so that he and Brutus can grow old together—friends in times of peace as in times of war. Though the battle has not even begun, Cassius says farewell to Brutus as though defeat were inevitable. He speaks with gentle resignation—almost as if he welcomes death.

Brutus, also convinced the end is near, says that suicide is against his philosophy, but that he would never suffer the indignity of being led, a prisoner, through the streets of Rome. Thus Brutus consciously denies his philosophy, and listens to his heart.

The two men part with a touching show of gentleness. Names and labels, roles and reputations—all fade in the face of death. The masks slip, and what we see is the simple humanity of two good friends.

ACT V, SCENE II

This brief scene indicates the passage of time, and lets us know that the battle has begun. Brutus seems confident and in control—a man of action as well as words. A moment ago his cause seemed lost; now fate is on his side as he takes the offense and orders Cassius to attack.

ACT V, SCENE III

Lines 1–50

The outcome of the battle remains uncertain: Brutus has beaten Octavius, but Cassius' troops are surrounded by Antony's. Cassius learns that Antony has set fire to his tents and sends his trusted friend Titinius to find out whether the approaching troops are friends or enemies. Cassius—the man who faulted Caesar for his physical imperfections—admits a handicap of his own: nearsightedness. He is shortsighted mentally as well as physically for he cannot see beyond the moment and assumes his death is near. "My life is run his compass," he says. His pessimism has no basis in fact, but he seems to want to believe the worst.

Pindarus reports that Titinius has been surrounded by the enemy and taken prisoner. Cassius calls himself a coward "to live so long,/To see my best friend ta'en before my face!" (lines 34–35). Shouting, "Caesar, thou art revenged," he stabs himself with the same sword that killed Caesar, and dies.

Cassius gains, at the moment of death, a certain dignity. Today we consider suicide a form of murder, but the Romans saw it as a noble act, particularly when it was done to avoid dishonor. Cassius' final thoughts are not for himself—for power or for glo-

ry—but for a friend whom he believes he has sent to
his death. Caesar, too, in his final moments, revealed
himself as a person who valued friendship above all.
Both Cassius and Caesar, facing death, focus upon
the importance of personal, private relationships,
rather than public reputation. This wins our affection;
it also wins our pity—for it comes too late to matter.

NOTE: **The Structure of the Play**   Some readers complain that *Julius Caesar* is a poorly constructed
play because one of the two main characters (Caesar)
dies before the end of the third act. Yet though Caesar
the man dies, his spirit continues to live in the hearts
of the people, and to dominate the action of the play.
His spirit revenges itself on Cassius—Brutus will be
next. What neither Cassius nor Brutus realizes is that
Caesarism cannot be destroyed so long as the people
need a powerful leader to give order and splendor to
their lives.

Lines 51–110

Titinius returns too late for Cassius to learn that
Brutus defeated Octavius, and that Titinius was not
taken prisoner but greeted by Brutus' triumphant
troops. How shortsighted of Cassius not to have con-
firmed his intelligence reports before taking his life!
On one hand, forces beyond his control—whether
coincidence or fate—have determined his destiny
and, therefore, the final outcome of the battle. On the
other hand, Cassius seems to have lost the will to fight
and thus brings about his own, and Brutus', destruction. Titinius compares Cassius' death to the setting
sun, which brings darkness to Rome:

> O setting sun,
> As in thy red rays thou dost sink to night,

So in his red blood Cassius' day is set.
The sun of Rome is set. Our day is gone:
                              Act V, Scene iii, lines 60–63

The tribute is sincere, we know, because Titinius now
takes his life to prove "how (he) regarded Caius Cassius." But how do we reconcile this picture of Cassius
with Caesar's portrait of him as a dangerous man with
a "lean and hungry look"? Perhaps the most we can
say is that Cassius—like the rest of us—was a different man to different people—as much a friend to
Titinius as an enemy to Caesar. It was Shakespeare's
genius that he could portray two sides (or more) of a
single person, without passing final judgment on
him. Can any of us claim such tolerance, understanding, or dramatic skill?

Brutus discovers the body of his fallen friend and
exclaims, "O Julius Caesar, thou are mighty yet!" Caesar the man has been slain, but his spirit continues to
rule.

Brutus calls Cassius "The last of all the Romans,"
adding,

It is impossible that ever Rome
Should breed thy fellow [equal].
                              Act V, scene iii, lines 100–101

Does his sorrow blind him to Cassius' faults? Is he
simply saying what is expected at the death of a
friend? Or does the finality of death restore his perspective on Cassius' good qualities? In any case, his
words imply that he believes as firmly as ever in the
rightness of his cause.

Note how Brutus feels he ought to cry, but, true to
his nature, is either so disciplined or so unfeeling that
he saves his tears for a more convenient moment. He

repeats himself—"I shall find time, Cassius; I shall find time" *(line 103)*—either because he is overcome with emotion, or because he doesn't mean what he's saying. Brutus wants the funeral to be held away from camp, "Lest it discomfort us" *(line 106)*. Either he really wants to protect the morale of his troops, or he is using them to hide his own discomfort. True to his nature, he puts aside whatever sorrow he feels and acts for the general welfare. "Let us to the field," he says, where "We shall try fortune in a second fight" *(line 110)*.

ACT V, SCENE IV

In this fallen world, people are still assuming other names and titles, and trying to be something they are not. Cato tries to live up to his father's reputation—"I am the son of Marcus Cato," he says—and is killed. (So his sister, Portia, insisted that she was Cato's daughter, too, and was rewarded with death.) Lucilius pretends to be Brutus, and Antony's soldiers take his word for it. Antony, however, is not fooled, and says:

> Keep this man safe;
> Give him all kindness. I had rather have
> Such men my friends than enemies.
> *Act V, Scene iv, lines 27-29*

Not long ago Antony was busy checking off the names of people who must die, so it's difficult to believe that he has suddenly developed a taste for mercy or a concern for the sanctity of human life. What he probably recognizes is his need to end the bloodshed if he is going to reestablish order and unite the people behind him. He may still be an opportunist, but he does seek reconciliation rather than revenge, which bodes well for the future of Rome.

ACT V, SCENE V

Lines 1–59

The tide has turned against Brutus. His scout, Statilius, reached the enemy lines but was killed or captured on his return. Brutus, sensing defeat, asks Dardanius, and then Volumnius, to slay him. The man of reason—who all his life has refused to succumb to his emotions–now breaks down and cries:

> Now is that noble vessel full of grief,
> That it runs over even at his eyes.
> *Act V, Scene v, lines 13–14*

Brutus' final moments seem almost joyful, without anger or regrets. He is still convinced of the justice of his cause, but welcomes death as a release from the trials of life. Like Cassius and Caesar, his final thoughts are not of Rome or of his own nobility, but of friendship:

> My heart doth joy that yet in all my life
> I found no man but he was true to me.
> *Act V, Scene v, lines 34–35*

Cassius, of course, was not true to Brutus when he sent him forged letters. And Antony was not true to Brutus when he promised not to blame the conspirators in his funeral oration. To the last, Brutus continues to see the best in people, and to make them seem better than they are; he also remains blind to human nature, and unable to see the world for what it is.

Brutus predicts *(lines 36–38)* that he will have more glory "by this losing day" than Octavius and Antony, but he is wrong again: Antony will soon become the first, and one of the greatest, emperors of Rome.

In his final words—"Caesar, now be still;/I killed not thee with half so good a will" *(lines 50–51)*—Brutus reveals that he has always been troubled by the assassination; that in his heart he is happier taking his own life than Caesar's. This is not necessarily an admission of wrongdoing, but it is an acknowledgment that he could not reconcile his love for Caesar with his public duty to assassinate him. Brutus, the man of reason, killed Caesar for the best interests of Rome; but Brutus, the man, has never forgiven himself for murdering a friend. Whether Brutus is to be praised or blamed for putting principles ahead of feelings is something every reader will have to decide for himself.

Lines 60–81

Octavius agrees to accept all of Brutus' men into his service—another indication of his willingness to heal wounds in order to reestablish order.

Antony's speech praising Brutus may be nothing more than a formal tribute to the dead. His words ring true only if he is saying that Brutus is the most noble of all the conspirators—not the most noble of all Romans.

Antony calls Brutus a person in whom the elements were so mixed "that nature might stand up/ And say to all the world, 'This was a man!' " *(lines 74–75).* Antony must be speaking of the public Brutus, and the mask he presented to the world; for the private man was haunted by ghosts, and "with himself at war" (Act I, Scene ii, line 46).

Octavius makes the final tribute, since with him the circle closes, and order is restored.

A STEP BEYOND

Tests and Answers

Test 1

1. Tribunes disperse the crowd as the play begins _B_
   A. in fear that the mob will riot
   B. fearing that Caesar's popularity may lead to the destruction of democracy in Rome
   C. upon the orders of the Senate

2. Caesar asks Antony to touch Calpurnia as he runs the race _C_
   A. to bring him luck
   B. as a signal to Caesar to refuse the crown
   C. to shake off her "sterile curse"

3. "Beware the Ides of March" was spoken by _A_
   A. a soothsayer to Caesar
   B. Cassius to Caesar
   C. Caesar to Brutus

4. "The fault, dear Brutus, is not in our _____, But in _____, that we are underlings." _____
   A. fate . . . leaders
   B. hands . . . our minds
   C. stars . . . ourselves

5. Cassius appeals to Brutus by _____
   I. pointing out Caesar's weaknesses
   II. offering Brutus the crown
   III. alluding to Brutus' noble ancestors

      A. I and II only
      B. II and III only
      C. I and III only

6. Caesar tells Antony that Cassius is dangerous _C_
   because
   A. he does not forget a grudge
   B. he is fat
   C. he seldom smiles

7. Immediately after Caesar refused the crown _____
   three times,
   I. there is a "tempest dropping fire as if
      there is strife in heaven"
   II. he suffered an epileptic fit
   III. he offered his throat to be cut
      A. I and II only
      B. II and III only
      C. I and III only

8. The conspirators want Brutus to join them _B_
   because
   A. Brutus' strength and courage would
      insure their success
   B. Brutus is highly regarded by the people
   C. they could more easily escape
      punishment if their plot failed

9. The message left in Brutus' window reads _B_
   A. "Peace, freedom and liberty!"
   B. "Speak, strike, redress!"
   C. "Think them as a serpent's egg and kill
      them in the shell!"

10. "Let us be sacrificers, but not butchers" was C
    an argument
    A. to prevent mutilating Caesar's body
    B. against killing Caesar
    C. against killing Antony

11. Was the assassination justified?

12. Who delivers the best funeral oration, Brutus or Antony?

13. What is Shakespeare's view of the common people of Rome? How do they help shape events?

14. What is Shakespeare's view of women?

Test 2

1. In his funeral oration, Antony refers to the   C
   assassins as
   A. traitors
   B. men of good cause
   C. honorable men

2. Caesar's will   B
   A. names Mark Antony as his
      successor
   B. leaves 75 drachmas to every
      Roman citizen
   C. explains why he refused the
      crown

3. After the funeral, the Plebeians   _____
   A. kill Cinna the poet, mistaking him for Cinna the conspirator
   B. vow to follow Mark Antony
   C. go to burn the houses of the assassins

4. Antony's opinion of Lepidus, his fellow member of the triumvirate, is that he is   B
   A. an honorable man, "high-spirited and meritorious"
   B. to be used as a beast of burden "to ease ourselves of sland'rous loads"
   C. to be feared because "such men are never at heart's ease Whiles they behold a greater than themselves"

5. At Sardis, Brutus' servant tells him that Cassius   *A*

   A. has shown himself to be "a hot friend cooling"
   B. is plotting to kill Brutus
   C. is planning to flee the country to escape the wrath of the populace

6. Following the argument over Cassius' refusal to give Brutus gold to pay his legions,   *C*

   A. they part in anger with the intention of fighting Antony with their separate armies
   B. Cassius explains that he himself is in financial straits
   C. are reconciled and attribute their rash statements to ill temper

7. Portia   *B*

   A. was killed by the mob that stormed Brutus' house
   B. died by swallowing fire
   C. tried to persuade Brutus to save himself by delivering Cassius to Antony

8. Brutus' argument for meeting the enemy at Philippi is   *C*

   A. he has received an omen in a dream that good fortune awaits him there
   B. that there his forces would be better rested and prepared
   C. that the opposing army will pick up strength and numbers if allowed to march from Philippi

9. The ghost of Caesar   *B*
   A. hurls at Brutus the accusation, "Et tu, Brute?"
   B. tells Brutus he shall see him at Philippi
   C. completes the prophetic song that Brutus' slave had begun before he fell asleep

10. Before the battle, Cassius says he saw the following omen: *B*
    A. a snake had wrapped itself around his army's ensign
    B. two eagles perched on his army's ensign were replaced by ravens and crows
    C. his army's ensign had fallen to the ground and was ripped to shreds by two lions

11. Is Julius Caesar a well-structured play?

12. Is Brutus a man of honor who is destroyed by forces beyond his control? Or is he a self-righteous hypocrite who cloaks his evil deeds in high-minded phrases and plunges his country into civil war?

13. Is Rome left in good hands after the death of Brutus?

14. What role does friendship play in the lives and destinies of the characters?

ANSWERS

Test 1

1. B	**2.** C	**3.** A	**4.** C	**5.** C	**6.** C
7. B	**8.** B	**9.** B	**10.** C		

11.   Critics have argued this point for hundreds of years, so you can defend either point of view as long as you support your case with evidence from the text.

If you think Caesar deserves to die, you'll need to prove that he's unfit to rule. That's not hard to do. Physically, he's partially deaf and suffers from epilepsy—the marks of an aging man seriously past his prime. As for his mental shortcomings, he's superstitious and (though he hides the truth from himself) he's afraid and easily flattered. His ambition threatens to undermine hundreds of years of Republican rule. His speech comparing himself to the North Star is the height of blasphemy and arrogance. His refusal to pardon Publius Cimber is the mark of a tyrant incapable of justice or pity. Even Caesar's close friend Brutus thinks Caesar must die—and Brutus, despite his shortcomings, is an honorable man who thinks only of his country's best interests.

If you believe the murder is wrong, you can find an equal amount of evidence to support your position. Caesar may have physical ailments, but so what? Hasn't he just returned triumphantly from battle? He may suffer from fears and superstitions, but so do all men: what he should be judged for are his accomplishments, not his private life. He may be ambitious, but what's wrong with ambition? No one has gotten anywhere without it. In our democratic age we're suspicious of politicians who seek unlimited power. But the Elizabethans lived under a strong monarch who brought them peace and prosperity; they would have had no such prejudice against Caesar. Nowhere in the play do we see Caesar suppressing the rights of the people. (He does put the Roman officers Flavius and Marullus to death, but they are traitors who deserve to die.) He is vain, but deserves to be vain. In his personal life he is considerate to his wife, courteous to the conspirators, and generous (in his will) to the Roman people. He can be inflexible, as when he refuses to pardon Publius Cimber, but the times demanded such behavior. *Julius Caesar* was written near the end of Elizabeth's reign, when Shakespeare and his contemporaries were deeply troubled by the threats to her life and by the need for an orderly succession. Shakespeare's play can be seen, therefore, as a defense of order, and a warning to his fellow-Elizabethans of the dangers of tyranny and revolution.

12. There is no right or wrong answer to the question. But like a good defense attorney you can gather your evidence from the facts (as presented in the text, Act III, Scene ii) and make a strong case for either point of view.

If you favor Brutus' speech, you can argue that: (1) it is spoken by a man who respects his audience and believes that truth is on his side; (2) Brutus reasons with people, he does not talk down to them or cater to their base emotions; (3) he is extremely effective in his use of rhetorical questions, questions that involve the people and encourage them to make up their own minds; (4) he is brief and to the point; (5) he convinces his audience (when Brutus finishes, the citizens exclaim, "This Caesar was a tyrant," and "We are blest that Rome is rid of him"); or (6) the only reason the crowds turn against Brutus is that Antony has the last word; the crowds would probably have turned against Antony if Brutus had been the last to speak.

If you think Antony made the most effective speech—and this is what most critics have argued over the years—you can point out that: (1) yes, Antony appeals to the emotions of his audience, but people are led by their emotions, not by their intellects; (2) Antony's speech seems more spontaneous and therefore more genuinely felt; he forms his words as he goes along, in response to the shifting moods of his audience; (3) Brutus seems to talk down to the people; Antony identifies with them; or (4) Brutus seems to be reading a memorized speech; Antony seems to speak from the heart.

When you defend Antony's speech, point out how he breaks down and cries and how he shows the crowds Caesar's bloody cloak. Point out that he speaks in verse (Brutus speaks in prose), and that he avoids fine distinctions, which the public cannot understand, and reduces everyone to heroes or villains. Mention that though he does appeal to the so-called baser instincts of his audience, he does so for what he considers a noble end.

For further help, turn to "The Play," Act III, Scene ii.

13.   Shakespeare's portrait of the common people is not very flattering. When we first see them, they're enjoying a day off from work to celebrate Caesar's triumphant return. Politics don't seem to interest them: they're too wrapped up in their own private lives to care about anything but their holiday. In his funeral oration, Brutus tries to reason with the people, but they misunderstand him and try to turn him into a Caesar. No intellectual argument is going to reduce their need for a leader; if Caesar the man is dead, they will find someone else to take his place. Antony succeeds in his speech because he appeals to the blind emotions of the crowd. When he finishes speaking, the crowds cry, "Revenge! About [let's go!]! Burn! Fire! Kill! Slay!" (*Act III, Scene ii, line 206*). Their murder of the innocent poet Cinna (*Act III, Scene iii*) reminds us how dangerous they can be when their emotions are unchecked. If you were going to compare the Roman populus to a single person, you would have to compare the common people to the body, and the rulers to the head. The assassination is justified by the need to continue a Republican (representative) form of government. But from what we see of the people, they lack the intelligence or interest to select rulers to represent them. What interests them are the trappings of greatness, the pageantry and the glory. Caesar is murdered to give these people their freedom, but it's doubtful that freedom is what they want or need.

14. You can write a strong paper arguing that Shakespeare's women are weak, subservient, and superstitious. And you can write an equally strong essay arguing that Shakespeare was hundreds of years ahead of his time in his view of woman as man's equal, perhaps even his "better half."

Let's start with the less flattering view of women. Calpurnia speaks only 26 lines, so you have no excuse for not reading them carefully. The second time she appears *(Act II, Scene ii)* she comes across as a frightened child haunted by bad dreams and omens. She is undignified, nervous, and weak. Living with Caesar has apparently not taught her how to deal with him, for she orders him not to leave the house—the surest way, of course, of forcing him to go. Portia asks to be treated as her husband's equal; when he does so, she falls apart and eventually takes her life. Note, too, that Portia wants to be Brutus' equal only so that she can be more a part of his life; nowhere does she suggest that he be more a part of hers.

If you want to write a paper portraying Shakespeare as a defender of women's rights, point out that all of Calpurnia's dreams, and all of Portia's fears, come true. Thus Shakespeare's women, in their intuitive way, seem closer to the truth than the men. Both Portia and Calpurnia have an innate sense of wisdom that lets them see through words to the very heart of things. Both women are also devoted wives, concerned about the well-being of their husbands. Calpurnia may seem a bit shrill, but who wouldn't be, with a pompous husband like Caesar? Portia is modest and tender, but she is also strong willed and dignified. She is one of the few characters in the play who use language to communicate their feelings, rather than to hide from them. If the men in *Julius Caesar* had listened to their women, the assassination would never have taken place, and Rome would never have been plunged into civil war.

Test 2

1. C   **2.** B   **3.** C   **4.** B   **5.** A   **6.** C

7. B   **8.** C   **9.** B   **10.** B

11.   You can argue that it isn't—but only if you believe that Caesar is the main character and that it's wrong for the main character to die in the middle of a play. In order to prove that Caesar is Shakespeare's "hero," point out that the play is named after him, and that a reader's feelings toward the assassination, which is the central action of the play, depend on his attitude toward Caesar.

If you believe that Caesar is the main character and that *Julius Caesar* is a well-structured play, point out that although Caesar dies in the third act, his spirit—what he stands for—dominates the action of the play from the opening scene until Brutus' death, and that it continues to live on in the person of Octavius. To prove that Caesarism lives after the man's death, discuss: the way the common people want and need a king, whoever he may be; the appearance of Caesar's ghost *(Act IV, Scene iii, lines 273–285)*; Cassius' comment as he dies: "Caesar, thou art revenged" *(Act V, Scene iii, line 45)*; Brutus' comment that he has seen Caesar's ghost again on the fields of Philippi *(Act V, Scene v, lines 16–19)*; and Brutus' dying words, "Caesar, now be still" *(Act V, Scene v, line 50)*.

If you consider Brutus the main character, you'll have no trouble arguing that Julius Caesar is a well-constructed play, since the action begins with Brutus' involvement in the plot and ends with his death and the eulogy over his body.

A play can be structured, of course, not only around characters, but also around certain actions. You can point out that the assassination, the pivotal action of the play, takes place in the very middle of *Julius Caesar (Act III, Scene i)*. Acts I and II lead up to the assassination, and Acts IV and V trace the consequences of the assassination. A more balanced structure would be hard to imagine.

12. As in life itself, it's possible to defend two opposing points of view.

If you believe Brutus is a man of high principles who is simply too good for the world he lives in, point out how he is defeated (a) by the underhandedness of Cassius; (b) by the blind emotions of the mob; (c) by Cassius' fatal error on the battlefield; and (d) by the common man's need for a king. To prove that Brutus has a conscience, note the fact that he hasn't the heart to watch races *(Act 1, Scene ii, lines 25–30)* while a tyrant threatens the freedom of his countrymen. Point out the high esteem in which he's held by both friend and foe, by Senators and commoners alike. (The conspirators know they can't win the common people to their cause without Brutus' support.) Note how Brutus alone, of all the conspirators, insists that Antony's life be spared and that Antony be allowed to speak at Caesar's funeral. Study Brutus' own oration as the work of a man who believes that right is on his side and that justice will prevail. Quote Brutus' speeches defending his honor (for example: "For let the gods so speed me, as I love/ The name of honor more than I fear death" *(Act 1, scene ii, lines 88–89)*. Today, in our post-Freudian world, we wonder if a truly virtuous man would need to call attention to his virtue. Yet it seems only natural for a man contemplating murder to defend himself, and it seems unfair to question Brutus' integrity when he expresses how he feels.

If you are feeling less kind to Brutus, you could write a paper proving that he is the villain of the play. Note how Cassius gets him to join the conspiracy by flattering him and appealing to his sense of family pride *(Act 1, Scene ii, lines 58–62, 158–161)*. Note how in his discussions with Cassius, both before and after the assassination, he is incapable of compromise and always insists on getting his way. Point out how Brutus begins his speech *(Act II, Scene i, lines 10–34)* with his mind already made up to murder Caesar ("It must be by his death"), and how he goes on to rationalize this decision with the most tenuous logic. His pride causes him to dismiss Cicero, even though Cicero is the most famous orator of the day. Brutus insists that he himself is honorable, but a truly noble man wouldn't need to go around making pompous speeches about it. Brutus likes to think of himself as a Stoic, who lives by reason alone; yet he's plagued by a guilty conscience, and, in his quarrel with Cassius, he is reduced to a squabbling child. Brutus' funeral oration shows how out of touch he is with the hearts and minds of the

people whom he says he wants to serve. In his unwilling-
ness to accept himself for what he is, Brutus is as vain and
dangerous as Caesar.

13.   To answer this question, you need only to read and
carefully study Octavius' words during his four appearances—a total of only 30 lines. He appears in Act IV, Scene i
and in Act V, Scene v.

When Octavius first appears he's checking off the names
of people who must die, and behaving as casually as someone checking off items on a laundry list. Unlike Brutus, he
has no qualms about murder, and he doesn't let principles
stand in the way of what he thinks is best for his cause. As
the head of Rome, he would therefore probably be a pragmatist and a man of action. He would be willing to sanction
any action that furthered the greater good of his country.
Whether he would be a man of vision is unclear, but he
would establish specific goals and get results.

Octavius tries to save Lepidus' life, not, apparently, from
any sense of mercy—only moments before he was willing
to kill Lepidus' brother—but from the belief that it would be
useful to have another "tried and valiant" soldier in his
ranks. Later on Octavius offers to take all of Brutus' men
into his service. Charity doesn't seem to be one of his virtues, though; what seems to motivate him is the practical
need to end the war and reunite the country under his single rule.

Octavius is a person who accepts the world for what it is
and does everything necessary to achieve his goals. His
methods may not be admirable, but they are effective. To
his credit, he seems more interested in preserving order
than in revenge. Blind ambition seems to be less a factor in

his decisions than a clear-sighted, single-minded drive to defend what he considers the best interests of Rome. Would Brutus the idealist have made a better ruler? To answer that question, you'll have to discuss Brutus' behavior before and after the assassination, and then decide whether you think a country needs a visionary at its helm, or a practical politician.

14.   Brutus, Cassius, Caesar—all three strut across the public stage, speaking grandly about power and principles. But underneath, what matters most to them is the loyalty of friends. It is an act of disloyalty—the murder of Caesar— that undermines the order of the world and plunges Rome into civil war. Disloyalty is like a disease that can threaten the health not only of individuals but of an entire nation. As death approaches, the three men come to recognize the truth, that friendship matters more than abstract principles or vain ambitions. Health is restored when Octavius takes command and extends a friendly hand to his enemies.

How should you discuss the role of friendship in the lives of these three men? Point out that Caesar's last words *(Act III, Scene i, line 77)* are not about the loss of glory, or about death, but about the disloyalty of his friend, Brutus. Mention that when Brutus puts his abstract sense of justice ahead of his love of Caesar, he rains destruction on himself, on his fellow-conspirators, and on all of Rome. His betrayal accomplishes nothing, for Caesarism—what Caesar represents—lives on in the hearts of the people, and is reborn in the person of Octavius. Brutus' final words *(Act V, Scene v, lines 50–51)* are an admission that he never forgave himself for murdering a friend.

Point out that almost everything Cassius does is motivated by a need for friendship, and by a desire to revenge himself on those who deny it. Why does he want to destroy Caesar? Because Caesar bears a grudge against him. Why does he always follow Brutus' advice, even when it's contrary to good sense? Because he's dependent on Brutus' affection. Cassius' final thoughts *(Act V, Scene iii, lines 34–35)* are not for himself—for power and glory—but for a friend whom he believes (mistakenly) he has sent to his death.

Term Paper Ideas

1. What is Caesarism? What are its advantages and disadvantages, according to the Senators, according to the common people of Rome, and according to you?

2. Why, at this moment in Roman history, does Caesarism seem inevitable?

3. Should people be judged by their intentions, by their actions, or by the results of their actions? Defend your point of view with specific reference to the characters in *Julius Caesar*.

4. What are Caesar's strengths and weaknesses as a ruler, as a husband, and as an ordinary citizen of Rome?

5. Why did Shakespeare choose to include the character Lucius in his play?

6. Discuss Casca. Is he a poorly drawn character, or are his apparent inconsistencies merely the different sides of a complex personality?

7. What light does the argument scene between Cassius and Brutus *(Act IV, Scene iii)* shed on their personalities? Was Brutus right to condemn Lucius Pella for accepting bribes? What moral issue is at stake here? What is Cassius' position? What is yours?

8. Who makes a better ruler, a pragmatist or a man of principle? Defend your position with specific references to the play.

9. Discuss Brutus' relationship with Cassius.

10. Why does Cassius always give in to Brutus' wishes?

11. How does Cassius get Brutus to join the conspiracy?

12. What are Cassius' own reasons for joining the conspiracy, and how do they compare to Brutus'?

13. How were Shakespeare's attitudes toward (a) women, (b) politics, (c) order, or (d) fate determined by the age in which he lived?

14. Discuss four occasions when characters try to manipulate each other through the use of flattery.

15. Why is the play called *Julius Caesar* and not *The Tragedy of Marcus Brutus?*

16. Is Cassius, as Caesar says, a dangerous man who thinks too much? Or is Brutus correct when he calls Cassius "the last of all the Romans"?

17. Is Brutus an honorable man or a hypocrite? Discuss his strengths and weaknesses.

18. Which of the characters would you vote for as president or support as king? Defend your position with reference to the text.

19. How does the first scene introduce most of the major issues of the play?

20. Some critics call *Julius Caesar* a problem play. What problems does it pose that remain unresolved?

21. Critics like to point out that *Julius Caesar* is a transitional play that lies between the history plays and the tragedies. How does it reflect the themes and structure of the histories; how does it look forward to the tragedies?

22. Who is the main character of *Julius Caesar?* Who is the hero?

23. Would you have joined the conspiracy? Defend your point of view with references to the text.

24. The Elizabethans looked to Roman times for lessons in how to live. What did *Julius Caesar* teach them?

25. Portia is sometimes considered a modern woman. In what sense is she modern; in what sense is she a product of the times in which she lives?

26. Compare Portia and Calpurnia—their personalities, their values, their relationships to their husbands.

27. Can good ever come from evil? Discuss the problem of the virtuous murder.

28. Compare the public and private lives of any major character.

29. Discuss *Julius Caesar* as a play about the different ways in which people use language.

30. Discuss the use of fire imagery.

31. What role does Fate play in the lives of the characters and in the final triumph of Octavius?

32. Discuss *Julius Caesar* as a study of ideals and the reality of politics.

33. Discuss the theme of order and disorder in the play.

34. Read Shakespeare's source material in *Plutarch's Lives*. What light does it shed on the characters and themes of the play?

35. Compare the characters and themes of *Julius Caesar* and either *Henry V* or *Antony and Cleopatra*.

Further Reading

CRITICAL WORKS

Here are just a few of the works that will help you understand *Julius Caesar*. Most of them should be available in your school or community libraries.

Auchincloss, Louis. "Caesar, the Tudor Monarch," in *Motiveless Malignity* (Boston: Houghton Mifflin, 1969), pp. 83–94.

Bloom, Allan, "The Morality of the Pagan Hero," in *Shakespeare's Politics* (New York: Basic Books, 1964), pp. 75–112.

Dean, Leonard F. *Twentieth Century Interpretations of Julius Caesar* (Englewood Cliffs: Prentice-Hall, 1968). A collection of nineteen essays on the play.

Foakes, R. A. "An Approach to *Julius Ceasar*," in the Signet edition of *Julius Caesar* (New York: Signet, 1963), pp. 193–211.

Goddard, Harold C. "Julius Caesar," in *The Meaning of Shakespeare* (Chicago: University of Chicago Press, 1960), Vol. 1, pp. 307–330.

Granville-Barker, Harley, "Julius Caesar," in *Prefaces to Shakespeare* (Princeton: Princeton University Press, 1946), Vol II, pp. 160–222.

Ludowyk, E. F. C. "Julius Caesar," in *Understanding Shakespeare* (Cambridge: Cambridge University Press, 1962), pp. 172–198.

Schanzer, Ernest. "Julius Caesar," in *The Problem Plays of Shakespeare* (New York: Schocken Books, 1963), pp. 10–70.

Spencer, T. J. B. *Shakespeare's Plutarch* (Baltimore: Penguin Books, 1968). The lives of Caesar, Brutus and Antony—the primary source for Shakespeare's play.

Traversi, D. A. "Julius Caesar," in *An Approach to Shakespeare* (Garden City: Doubleday, 1956), pp. 492–512.

Traversi, D. A. "Julius Caesar," in *Shakespeare: The Roman Plays* (Stanford: Stanford University Press, 1963), pp. 21–75. This is an expanded version of the material that appears in *An Approach to Shakespeare*.

Van Doren, Mark. "Julius Caesar," in *Shakespeare* (Garden City: Doubleday Anchor, 1953).

Wright, Louis B. *Shakespeare for Everyman* (New York: Washington Square Press, 1964).

AUTHOR'S OTHER WORKS

Shakespeare wrote 37 plays (38 if you include *The Two Noble Kinsmen*) over a 20-year period, from about 1590 to 1610. It's difficult to determine the exact dates when many were written, but scholars have made the following intelligent guesses about his plays and poems:

Plays

1588–93	*The Comedy of Errors*
1588–94	*Love's Labor's Lost*
1590–91	*2 Henry VI*
1590–91	*3 Henry VI*
1591–92	*1 Henry VI*
1592–93	*Richard III*
1592–94	*Titus Andronicus*
1593–94	*The Taming of the Shrew*
1593–95	*The Two Gentlemen of Verona*
1594–96	*Romeo and Juliet*
1595	*Richard II*
1594–96	*A Midsummer Night's Dream*
1596–97	*King John*

1596–97	*The Merchant of Venice*
1597	*1 Henry IV*
1597–98	*2 Henry IV*
1598–1600	*Much Ado About Nothing*
1598–99	*Henry V*
1599	*Julius Caesar*
1599–1600	*As You Like It*
1599–1600	*Twelfth Night*
1600–01	*Hamlet*
1597–1601	*The Merry Wives of Windsor*
1601–02	*Troilus and Cressida*
1602–04	*All's Well That Ends Well*
1603–04	*Othello*
1604	*Measure for Measure*
1605–06	*King Lear*
1605–06	*Macbeth*
1606–07	*Antony and Cleopatra*
1605–08	*Timon of Athens*
1607–09	*Coriolanus*
1608–09	*Pericles*
1609–10	*Cymbeline*
1610–11	*The Winter's Tale*
1611–12	*The Tempest*
1612–13	*Henry VIII*

Poems

1592	*Venus and Adonis*
1593–94	*The Rape of Lucrece*
1593–1600	*Sonnets*
1600–01	*The Phoenix and the Turtle*

The Critics

On Shakespeare

In approaching Shakespeare, we must remember that he wrote, not for a small group of intellectuals, but for every man, from courtier to apprentice, for the man in the street, for anyone who could be lured to pay a penny or a tuppence to get into the theatre to see a play. Shakespeare wrote with one or both eyes on the box office. He wanted to be popular and he tried to write in such a manner and on such themes that Everyman would welcome his efforts—and pay for them.

—*Louis B. Wright*, Shakespeare for Everyman *1964*

On Omens

"He is a dreamer; let us leave him: pass," says Caesar, dismissing the Soothsayer who called out to him "Beware the ides of March." The event showed that he dismissed him at his peril. Shakespeare was growing more convinced that we neglect dreams and dreamers at our peril. He was a humanist, to be sure, and remained one to the end of his days. But from *Julius Caesar* on, his greater characters and greater plays are touched with the dream-light and dream-darkness of something that...transcends the merely human....The secret of human life, [Shakespeare] seems to say, lies beyond...life as well as within it.

—*Harold C. Goddard*, The Meaning of Shakespeare, *1960*

On Caesar

Caesar, unlike other Shakespearean characters who suffer from ambition, never says he wants the crown. But even if he did, would it seem so wicked to an Englishman, living under the rule of Elizabeth, that a man already at the helm of state should seek to be King? We know from the historical plays that Shakespeare thought it wrong to usurp a crown, but Caesar would not have been usurping one. What the Senate planned to offer him was only the outward and visible form of a power he already enjoyed.

It has also been argued that Caesar is shown in the play as an arrogant and unyielding man who has the soul of a despot and who could reasonably be expected to trample any remaining liberties of the Romans under his feet. Of course, the pomposity of Caesar's speeches offers some support for this, but I doubt that Shakespeare intended Caesar to be as pompous as his part reads to a twentieth-century eye. It is true that he sometimes speaks of himself in the third person, which has a grandiloquent ring in a nonmonarch, but he is the undoubted ruler of a great empire, and Shakespeare may have considered this form of expression perfectly fitting. He allows many rulers in his plays to take themselves very seriously indeed without seeming to denigrate them. What seems pompous to us, accustomed as we are to the compulsive humility of our own political candidates, may have appeared to Elizabethans as the gravity and majesty expected of a chief of state.

Caesar's statements about Cassius and his distrust of thin men are frequently read as the mutterings of a dictator who cannot abide the least independence of thought. But Caesar has every justification for distrusting Cassius, who is already plotting his murder, and he puts his finger on Cassius' primary motive, which is simple envy.

—*Louis Auchincloss*, Motiveless Malignity, *1969*

The essential greatness of Caesar being thus assumed, Shakespeare is free to exhibit in him human weaknesses apparently inconsistent with it. There are many advantages in this method of presentation. It gives reality to Caesar, the man; it suggests that Caesar's spirit is mightier than his person, a suggestion which is essential to the unity of the play; it enables the dramatist to present him in flesh and blood without reducing in stature the men who murder him; finally, it permits the audience to sympathise with Brutus just sufficiently to give poignancy to the disaster which overtakes him.

This last point is of major dramatic importance. The play could not easily have risen to the level of tragedy if Caesar had been portrayed consistently in full majesty. The conspiracy must then have inevitably impressed the audience as no more than a stupid plot contrived by a group of self-seeking politicians under the leadership of a misguided political crank. Such, in effect, it was, but the skillful dramatist, if he is to retain the sympathetic attention of his audience, will not obtrude the fact, but allow it to become fully apparent only at the close.

The infirmities of Caesar are not inventions of the dramatist. They are in part historical and in part derived from Plutarch's delight in the foibles of great men and his tendency to find such foibles more pronounced in his Roman heroes than in the heroes of his native Greece.

> —*John Palmer, "The Character of Caesar," from* Political Characters of Shakespeare, *reprinted in* Shakespeare: Julius Caesar, *1969*

Perhaps more than any other figure in history, Julius Caesar has evoked a divided response in the minds of those who have written about him. Indeed, it would not be an exaggeration to say that such a response, made up of attraction and repulsion, admiration and hostility, was the prevailing one among informed and educated men throughout Antiquity, the Middle Ages, and the Renaissance, so that we can speak of it as forming a tradition extending from Caesar's own day down to that of Shakespeare.

In Plutarch's attitude towards Caesar dislike and admiration mingle....However divided in his attitude toward Caesar, Plutarch's prevailing opinion seems to have been that his offences were committed under the influence of bad friends and against his better nature and that, although his motives were unworthy, his influence upon the state of Rome was largely beneficial.

In a sense, all that Shakespeare does is to dramatize the views of Caesar and the conspirators which he found in his 'sources', and especially Plutarch, distributing what are the divided and contradictory responses of a single writer among several characters who take different sides....

—*Ernest Schanzer*, The Problem Plays of Shakespeare, *1963*

On Brutus

Brutus is humorlessly good. If his duty is to know himself, his performance fails. Nobility has numbed him until he cannot see himself for his principles. When his principles are expressing themselves they are beautiful in their clarity; but when he speaks to himself he knows not who is there; he addresses a strange audience, and fumbles. . . . Shakespeare has done all that could be done with such a man, but what could be done was limited. . . . He is not mad, or haunted, or inspired, or perplexed in the extreme. He is simply confused.

—*Mark Van Doren*, Shakespeare, *1953*

Shakespeare's sympathy with Brutus does not imply approval of the murder of Caesar; it only means that he ultimately finds the spiritual problem of the virtuous murderer the most interesting thing in the story. Brutus best interprets the play's theme: Do evil that good may come, and see what does come!

—*Harley Granville-Barker*, Prefaces to Shakespeare, *Vol. 11, 1946*

In Brutus, then, Shakespeare discovered the noble hero with a tragic flaw. By that discovery he made it possible for English tragedy to reach a greatness hitherto attained only by Greek tragedy. All his tragedies written after *Julius Caesar* benefited by the discovery.

Julius Caesar is a landmark not merely in the history of Shakespearean tragedy but in the history of English tragedy. Before Brutus there had been no tragic hero on the English stage whose character had combined noble grandeur with fatal imperfection.

> —*William Farnham, " 'High-minded*
> *Heroes' from Shakespeare's Tragic*
> *Frontier," reprinted in* Shakespeare:
> Julius Caesar, 1969

On Cassius

Cassius, the man of passion, is set in strong contrast to Brutus, the philosopher.

An egoist certainly; yet not ignobly so, seeking only his own advantage. Convinced in a cause— as we find him convinced; that Caesar's rule in Rome must be free Rome's perdition—he will fling himself into it and make no further question, argue its incidental rights and wrongs no more, as Brutus may to weariness.

Egoist he is, yet not intellectually arrogant. He sees in Brutus the nobler nature and a finer mind, and yields to his judgment even when he strongly feels that it is leading them astray.

> —*Harley Granville-Barker*, Prefaces to
> Shakespeare, *Vol. 11, 1946*

On The Two Funeral Orations

Editor after editor has condemned Brutus' speech as poor and ineffective, and most of them have then proceeded to justify Shakespeare for making it so. It is certainly not meant to be ineffective, for it attains its end in convincing the

crowd. Whether it is poor oratory must be to some
extent a matter of taste. Personally, accepting its
form as one accepts the musical convention of a
fugue, I find that it stirs me deeply. I prefer it to
Antony's. It wears better. It is very noble prose.

One may so analyze [Antony's] speech
throughout and find it a triumph of effective clev-
erness. The cheapening of the truth, the appeals to
passion, the perfect carillon of flattery, cajolery,
mockery and pathos, swinging to a magnificent
tune, all serve to make it a model of what popular
oratory should be. In a school for demagogues its
critical analysis might well be an item in every
examination paper. That is one view of it. By
another, there is nothing in it calculated or false.
Antony feels like this; and, on these occasions, he
never lets his thoughts belie his feelings, that is all.
And he knows, without stopping to think, what
the common thought and feeling will be, where
reason and sentiment will touch bottom—and it if
be a muddy bottom, what matter!—because he is
himself, as we said, the common man raised to the
highest power. So, once in touch with his audience, he can hardly go wrong.

—*Harley Granville-Barker*, Prefaces to
Shakespeare, *Vol. 11, 1946*

[Brutus' speech] is one of the worst speeches
ever made by an able and intelligent man. Its sym-
metrical structure, its balanced sentences, its
ordered procedure, its rhetorical questions, its
painfully conscious and ornamental style, its
hopelessly abstract subject matter, all stamp it as
the utterance of a man whose heart is not in his
words. It is a dishonest speech.

The cry of the Third Citizen, "Let him be Caesar," measures its practical effectiveness. Those
four words have often been pointed out as one of
the most crushing ironies in the play. They are,
and with the other comments of the populace
show how hopeless the cause of the conspirators
was. These people did not deserve liberty. They
were ready for slavery.

Antony's speech, on the other hand, for all its playing on the passions of the people, and for all its lies, is at bottom an honest speech, because Antony loved Caesar. Because to that extent he has the truth on his side, he is as concrete as Brutus was abstract. A sincere harangue by a demagogue is better than the most "classic" oration from a man who speaks only with his lips.

—*Harold C. Goddard*, The Meaning of Shakespeare, 1960

On The Assassination

We shall notice throughout it a strong distrust of subversion and conspiracy. These were, in the knowledge and experience of all Elizabethans, the greatest disruptions of the state. The *Homilies:* appointed to be read in churches throughout the realm, have already been mentioned. Shakespeare not only knew these; he apparently accepted their instruction. In them he would have found the lesson driven home that conspiracy is dangerous, that it is never to be trusted, and that directed against the king or ruler it is both against God's commandment and doomed to create confusion involving both conspirators and the country. It could be nothing but evil. . . .It is probably with a mind made up on these points that Shakespeare read Plutarch and wrote his play

—*E. F. C. Ludowyk*, Understanding Shakespeare, 1962

Caesar's death is followed by a civil war in which Shakespeare must have seen a parallel to the Wars of the Roses that had so obsessed his earlier years. Certainly we know that Shakespeare stood for civil order above everything, and Caesar's death was followed by the destruction of the existing order.

—*Louis Auchincloss*, Motiveless Malignity, 1969

On Casca

I am going to risk a generalisation about Shakespeare. He was an Elizabethan dramatist, and I do not think the Elizabethans were conscientious over their characters; they would often alter them in the middle in order to get on with the play. Beaumont and Fletcher contain glaring examples of this. Good men become bad and then good again; traitors turn into heroes and vice versa without any internal justification. And Shakespeare scmetimes does it too. There is an example—not a glaring one—in this play, in the character of Casca. Casca first appears as extremely polite and indeed servile to Caesar, 'Peace ho! Caesar speaks,' he cries. Then he shows himself to Brutus and Cassius as a sour blunt contradictious fellow, who snaps them up when they speak and is grumpy when they invite him to supper. You may say this is subtlety on Shakespeare's part, and that he is indicating that Casca is a dark horse. I don't think so. I don't think Shakespeare was bothering about Casca—he is merely concerned to make the action interesting and he alters the character at need. Later on, during the thunderstorm, Casca becomes different again; he walks about with a drawn sword, is deeply moved by the apparitions, and utters exalted poetry. At the murder-scene he wounds Caesar in the neck, and then we hear of him no more. His usefulness is over.

> —*E. M. Forster*, Two Cheers for
> Democracy, *reprinted in* Shakespeare:
> Julius Caesar, *1969.*